# VISIONS &
# LONGINGS

*Medieval Women Mystics*

MONICA FURLONG

SHAMBHALA
*Boston*
*1997*

Shambhala Publications, Inc.
Horticultural Hall
300 Massachusetts Avenue
Boston, Massachusetts 02115
http://www.shambhala.com

9  8  7  6  5  4  3  2  1

First Paperback Edition
Printed in the United States of America
⊗ This edition is printed on acid-free paper that meets the
American National Standards Institute Z39.48 Standard.
Distributed in the United States by Random House, Inc.,
and in Canada by Random House of Canada Ltd

The Library of Congress catalogues the hardcover edition
of this book as follows:

Furlong, Monica.
Visions and longings: medieval women mystics/
Monica Furlong.—1st ed.
p.  cm.
ISBN 1-57062-125-X (alk. paper)
ISBN 1-57062-314-7 (pbk.)
1. Mysticism.  2. Mysticism—Europe—History—Middle Ages,
600–1500.  3. women mystics—Europe.  I. Title.
BV5077.E85F87  1996                          95-48804
248.2'2'09224—dc20                               CIP

Let your women keep silence in the churches:
for it is not permitted unto them to speak.
—I CORINTHIANS 14:34

*In memory of, and gratitude for, all the women
who did not keep silent in the churches.*

# CONTENTS

# PREFACE

MANY WOMEN besides the ones included here had mystical experiences, wrote about them, and were regarded as leaders in the period I have chosen for this book. I picture them collectively as a translucent wave gathering itself slowly and tentatively in the eleventh century, rising swiftly in the twelfth and thirteenth centuries, reaching a magnificent crescendo in the fourteenth.

The choice of which women to include was partly practical, as translations into English from the medieval dialects used by the women were in some cases not available, partly idiosyncratic, as I felt more drawn to one woman than another or felt that one revealed traits that were particularly interesting. Julian, the mystic with whom I have finished the book, is the one who speaks most clearly to me in her love and comprehending sanity and in the originality and genius of her mind.

I took a liberty with the title of the book by including Héloïse, who is not a mystic. She seemed to belong in it from my first thoughts about the subject, and when I later had doubts and tried to leave her out, it felt wrong. I think this is because, with her passionate commitment to a human lover, Abelard, and to sexuality, she forms a contrast, a counterpoint, to the passionate and celibate religious ardor of the other women. And perhaps she belongs with them because, unusual among women of her period, she had a strong underlying conviction of her own worth. I particularly like her cry to Abelard, "Wholly guilty though I am, I am, as you know, wholly innocent." Here is a woman who trusts her own convictions more than she trusts the verdict of authority—as, to varying degrees, do all the women in this book.

# INTRODUCTION

"ALL MYSTICS SPEAK the same language and come from the same country."[1] This is perhaps not quite true. Women mystics, or at any rate the ones examined in this book, come, if not from a different country, at least from a different province of the mystical country, and their language has different idioms and inflections. What they and their male counterparts have in common, though, is the conviction that there is a reality, a profound meaning, behind or beyond or within the world of appearances. Most, perhaps all, of us have this sense at times, but for the mystics their relationship, their intimacy, with this meaning, and their longing to be united to it, is the most important one of their lives. They often give the word *God* to that reality. Visions draw them toward it, and the visions create further yearning, a vocation to give up their lives to the search for it, whatever the incidental hardships. None of them better expresses the yearning than Angela di Foligno, flinging herself upon the pavement of the church at Assisi and crying out in agony, "Love unknown. Why, why, why?" She, like the other women in this book, had an overpowering need to discover the answer.

Christian mystics speak of this movement of discovery as the "Unitive Way," a journey that brings them into a sense of oneness with God or Christ. They embark on it by way of the Purgative Way (a means of ridding themselves of whatever blocks their approach to God) and the Illuminative Way, a stage in which they are taught by their visions. They travel by way of meditation and contemplation, by symbolic actions of a very individual kind—Christina, as a young girl, making a little mark with her finger on the door of Saint Albans Abbey; Clare, on her way to join Francis of Assisi, leaving her father's house by way of "the door of the dead"; Angela di Foligno stripping off her clothes in front of a crucifix; Catherine of Siena cutting off her hair as a refusal of marriage—as well as by a number of better-known religious routes: fasting, illness, pain, loneliness, abstinence from intimate human relationships.

So strange is this path in the light of much twentieth-century thought that it takes a particular sort of generosity on our part to open ourselves to the mystics' way of looking at the world; we have to overcome our fear of approaching people who strike us as bizarre and extraordinarily unlike ourselves and maybe recognize that, in associating with the mystics, there *is* a kind of danger. We are forced to consider ways of thought that are strange to our culture. It is a temptation to defend ourselves by attaching psychological labels, and this must be resisted—and yet at the same time it seems proper to apply what we know of human conduct and its roots to sift what is genuine from what is purely pathological in writers who reveal many traits of mental disturbance. It is a considerable dilemma.

So there is both daring and difficulty in entering the minds of the mystics, an inner stretching that perhaps otherwise happens to us only as we struggle with great art. A number of commentators, Evelyn Underhill among them, suggest that mystics tend to appear in periods of high civilization, that they are themselves a flowering of it.

I have already said that this book is about one province of the country of mysticism, or rather it is about one district within that province, the district of medieval women. It further confines itself to one smaller area—women most of whom became famous as mystics in the high medieval period. It begins in the late eleventh century, with Hildegard in Germany and Christina of Markyate in England, and ends with Margery Kempe and Julian of Norwich in fourteenth-century England.

All these women are doubly interesting; they are mystics and they are also among the first very few women in Europe whose writing or dictation has come down to us and from whom, therefore, we can learn firsthand something of what their lives were like. There are some earlier texts by women—Perpetua's testimony before her martyrdom, for example, or Hrotsvit's plays, and there are women writers who are known to us mainly by legend, such as Sappho. There are certainly earlier women religious leaders, some of them very distinguished, such as Hilda of Whitby.

But now, suddenly, around the eleventh and twelfth centuries, many more women become what the Epistles of Paul and the Fathers thought women should not be— audible and visible—writing with intelligence and passion and telling us about their lives and ideas with extraordinary vehemence and energy. One of these very early stories is a remarkable tale of adventure. Christina, first known as Theodora (b. ca. 1096–98), a child of well-to-do parents in Huntingdonshire, England, having decided almost as a child that she wanted to enter a convent, is brutally forced by her parents into a marriage that will add to their prosperity. Christina, as she now calls herself, refuses to consummate the marriage and eventually escapes, taking refuge in a hermit's cell and, as time goes on, becoming a recluse herself.

Her story, told with a sort of high spirits reminiscent of girls' school stories of the 1920s and 1930s (perhaps because they in turn described a later attempt by women to be freer and live more adventurous lives), also indicates the degree to which a medieval woman was a chattel in her father's home. Christina's father, Autti, complains bitterly to the local monks that his pride will be damaged if his daughter does not go through with the marriage he has forced on her, and they, together with the local bishop, clearly think the girl is being tiresome. The whole story demonstrates Christina's courage and determination and the way that her love of God makes it possible for her, a young girl with almost everyone against her, to emerge into a kind of autonomy almost unimaginable at the beginning of the story.

Their relationships with God, and often enough little else in their situation, also made it possible for the other women in this book, each in her different way, to emerge from the shadows to which they were condemned by misogyny and become public people.

"By acknowledging the pervasiveness of medieval misogyny," said the American literary scholar Elizabeth Petroff, "we value more highly the literary gifts necessary for the emergence of the women writers in this period, and we can better understand the great risk an individual woman took in becoming visible as a spiritual leader."[2]

The women well knew the danger of their visibility. Christina incurred the wrath of Robert Bloet, bishop of Lincoln, and only felt reasonably safe after his death. She achieved the single life she wanted only by "disappearing" for several years and living in circumstances of appalling hardship. Hildegard, seeking to set up her own religious foundation at Rupertsberg, had a frightening quarrel with the Benedictine abbot of Disibodenberg and a bitter struggle to secure the financial assets needed for the task. Mechthild of Magdeburg speaks openly about her fear that because of her "book"—*The Flowing Light*—she may suffer death by burning.

Fifty years after Mechthild, her fellow Beguine Marguerite Porete *was* burned because she would not renounce her book *The Mirror of Simple Souls* in 1310, and the Beguines were condemned at the Council of Vienne the following year. Clare, though admired by clergy and popes, had a lifelong battle to establish the kind of *forma vitae* for women religious that she thought was appropriate to them, and she only received the papal bull accepting her ideas on her deathbed. In her joy she was seen to kiss the document again and again.

Margery Kempe's paranoia perceived persecution everywhere, but she did run perilously close to charges of heresy several times and was briefly imprisoned. Julian of Norwich must have known that her questioning of eternal damnation made her vulnerable at a time when a number of heresy hunts were raging. Grace Jantzen points out that Julian's cell lay in sound and smell, if not in sight, of "the

Lollard pit" in Norwich where many heretics were burned to death.[3]

The women managed to survive, either because of the friendship and patronage of influential clerics, because they belonged to or were associated with powerful religious orders, or because they were particularly skillful at steering their fragile craft among the rocks and whirlpools of the medieval church. Their own strength of character carried them through terrifying vicissitudes.

Studying them we gradually discover that their inner pressures—both spiritual and psychological—became so urgent that they overrode fear and convention. They couldn't "not speak," any more than they could force themselves into the mold prescribed for contemporary women.

So what was it that drove them? "The [medieval] women's motivation for writing at all" says the scholar Peter Dronke "seems rarely to be predominantly literary: it is often more urgently serious than is common among men writers; it is a response springing from inner needs, more than from an artistic, or didactic, inclination." Dronke notes that the women's writing is not like the men's. It has a quality he described as "immediacy." "They look at themselves more concretely and more searchingly than many of the highly accomplished men writers who were their contemporaries. This immediacy can lend women's writing qualities beside which all technical flawlessness is pallid."[4]

The immediacy brought women many male as well as female readers; there was a good deal of novelty interest in the women's work, and in any case fewer women than men could read. *The Mirror of Simple Souls*, heretical or not, was read widely across Europe and may have influenced Meister Eckhart; Angela di Foligno's *The Book of the Experience of the Truly Faithful*, with its thirty steps toward the divine encounter (a kind of do-it-yourself mystical textbook), made her a cult figure in her own lifetime; Mechthild of Magdeburg's *The Flowing Light of the Godhead* is thought to have been important to Dante. Yet many of the women tended to be forgotten after their own lifetime (or, worse still, it was claimed that their works were written by men). Only in recent years, with attempts to redress the silencing of women's voices in history, have many of these writings begun to be rediscovered and re-translated.

Apart from the peculiarly driven quality of the women mystics and their need to communicate what it was they saw in their visions, there were other reasons that their voices should suddenly have been heard after so many centuries of silence.

The most important one was the increasing use of the vernacular. Before the middle of the twelfth century, books were written in Latin, not in a writer's familiar tongue. A very few women—Héloïse, Beatrijs of Nazareth, Hadewijch—had the sort of education that enabled them to write Latin as well as any male scholar. Héloïse's contemporary, Hildegard, wrote it with awkwardness. She was born too early to take advantage of the fashion of using the vernacular. At a period when it was an unusual achievement for women to read or, more difficult, write, the possibility of using one's mother tongue to express ideas was very liberating.

Or it may be that women simply reaped the benefit of a general democratization of ideas, with many people who could not write Latin, not only women, finding they had things they wanted to say publicly. Some heretical groups—the Lollards, for instance—used the vernacular to expound their ideas. It followed that ecclesiastical authorities were wary or even downright suspicious of those who wrote in the vernacular—it allowed self-expression to those outside the clerical world.

Not all the women in this book could read or write. Christina of Markyate was unable to tell us her exciting life story directly; she dictated it, or at any rate told it, to an unknown scholar, possibly Abbot Thomas De La Mare of Saint Albans, who wrote it down carefully.

In contrast, the Beguines of the Low Countries wrote in Low German, Flemish, and Dutch. (It is interesting that Beatrijs of Nazareth, despite her Latin scholarship, wrote in dialect Flemish; perhaps what these women wished to say went best in the vernacular.) Catherine of Siena is thought to have taught herself to read during the period when her parents confined her to the house for refusing to marry. Because her early letters are dictated and the later ones are not, it is deduced that later in her life she learned to write. Catherine wrote in the Sienese dialect; Angela dictated in Umbrian dialect; Julian of Norwich wrote in Middle English. Margery Kempe was obliged to dictate her Booke. The first amanuensis she chose just wrote down a lot of squiggles that could not be deciphered by anyone, a painful experience of the humiliation and frustration of illiteracy, since Margery longed to be heard, as well as to be able to read spiritual books.

Perhaps the lack of academic influence and pretension, and the use of the mother tongue in women's writing, accounted in part for the "immediacy" of which Dronke writes. Certainly there is a sense of both psychological release and urgency of expression. The pressure of the visions compelled the visionary, often timidly, to share what had been seen and understood. "I am a poor little woman," Mechthild of Magdeburg says, "but I write this book out of God's heart and mouth."

In medieval times claims of visionaries were treated with considerable respect, and even the fact that these particular visionaries were women did not nullify that, mostly, one must assume, because of the quality of the women themselves, which was often as eloquent as their writing. There is also a persistent Christian idea that God often chooses humble instruments to teach important lessons, and this worked in the women's favor or at least gave them the benefit of the doubt.

Visions, and the quality of life out of which it was believed such visions came, also gave the women status as prophets, both in the wider sense of permitting them to make criticisms of church and society—of corrupt clergy or religious, for instance—and in the narrower sense of their being able to predict the future, almost as a fortune-teller might, a gift respected and valued in medieval times. Christina amazes her friend Geoffrey of Saint Albans by always knowing when he is due to arrive on a visit (William Blake's friends, six centuries later, noted the same gift in the mystical poet), and she had a disconcerting way of detecting lewd or violent thoughts in her visitors. Margery also had the gift of knowing things about the future.

Because of their visionary and prophetic qualities, the women were influential in their private lives as well as in their newfound public personae. Margery's rude and disobedient son returned from a stay in Europe a changed man, changed, he said, because of her prayers. The Spiritual Franciscan Ubertino da Casale, describing the influence of Angela di Foligno upon him, said, "No one who had known me before could doubt that the spirit of Christ was begotten anew within me through her," and his words were echoed by friends and disciples of many another holy woman. Julian, who counseled many in Norwich in a time of acute social unrest, was left bequests in a number of wills, presumably by people who had used and valued her ministry.

The most public of them all in terms of influence was Catherine of Siena, a woman from a working-class background—her father was a dyer and her mother possibly a washerwoman—who, in the struggles between the Italian city-states and the papacy, tried to make peace between Florence and Pope Gregory XI. She is thought to have been instrumental in persuading the pope to return to Rome from Avignon. There is a sense of great strength about Catherine, and also of severity, a severity expressed as much in the hard life she imposed on herself as in some of her utterances about others. From our own place in time, where it is still the case that relatively few women exercise political or diplomatic or ecclesiastical power, we can wonder at how extraordinary Catherine's achievement was.

Despite the profound influence exerted by these women, they were, like all women of their time, disabled and humiliated by a sense of their stigmatization within Christianity—that is to say, the stigmatization of women as a class, regardless of their individual qualities. Part of the stigma had to do, as many writers have noted, with the identification of women with nature, men, by contrast, being identified with mind or spirit. It began early in Christian history. In his book about sexual renunciation in early Christianity, Peter Brown describes how, as early as the second century, the Christian church had developed a distinct and heroic identity for itself. Some of that heroism was demonstrated in a valiant endurance of persecution, some in an extraordinary mastery of bodily appetites. While the contemporary world set great value on sexual fulfillment, for men, that is (Brown points out that a favorite euphemism in Greek for the penis was "the necessity"), the early Christians were prepared to demonstrate that with the help of their belief, the body's sexual and other needs—food, rest—could be transcended. By abstinence from sexual intercourse, a radical overcoming of the body was achieved, helped on its way by a prevailing belief that the world was shortly to end, so that at least one reason for sexual intercourse, that of having children, became pointless.

"Continence," says Brown, paraphrasing Tertullian, "the suspension of all future sexual activity, brought down the gift of the Spirit: 'By continence you will buy up a great stock of sanctity, by making savings on the flesh, you will be able to invest in the Spirit.' "[5]

This powerful sense of the spiritual power of celibacy, and the particular power of those who remained virgins, continued strongly into the Middle Ages and beyond; indeed, Christianity retains vestiges of the conviction to this day. In the early centuries it was bound up with a prophetic radicalism, the young Church wanting to separate its members both from a life of hedonism and sexual promiscuity, for which some cities and cults in the Mediterranean were well known, and from something less extreme, what we might call a bourgeois world of comfortable family life indifferent to the claims of the spirit. Christians were different. They lived with one foot in eternity, prepared, like Perpetua, to sacrifice the claims of husband, newborn child and family, and finally life itself, to prophesy for Christ. One way even those not called to martyrdom could witness to the new life was to renounce what to others was uniquely precious—their sexuality.

This idea was, in different forms, widespread among the early Christian churches. Brown says of the Syrian churches that "high hopes gathered around the gesture of sexual renunciation: to have renounced sexual activity meant something more than to have brought sexual urges under control by rigorous self-discipline. Renunciation and baptism into the Church declared the power of sex null and void. Possession of the Holy Spirit conferred by baptism was thought to lift men and women above the vast 'shame' of the human condition."[6]

Tertullian describes young girls in the Carthaginian church trying to overcome the stigma of being female by deciding to remain unmarried, feeling that this gave the right to stand bareheaded and without a veil, the symbol of women's "shame." In Tertullian's eyes, however, they were mistaken in supposing that even voluntary virginity might transcend their shame. On the contrary, he thought, women were seductive by their very nature, and even Christian baptism could not overcome this.

Not all Christians took the route of sexual abstinence, but the feeling that it was "a better way" gradually gained ground. In this oblique way, if in no other, misogyny entered Christian attitudes. Prolonged or lifelong abstinence from sexual relations by men made women seem strange,

lurid, dangerous, the subjects of fantasy, some of it porno-
graphic, much as it has often more recently been claimed
happens in all-male societies—schools, universities, armies. No doubt homosexual fear as well as distaste for
women also came into play. Women were "the Flesh" (and
as such at war with "the Spirit"), or "Nature," both words
being synonymous with temptation. Clement of Alexandria (third century) thought "the very awareness of her
own nature must arouse a sense of shame in woman."

The dangerousness of women was personified by refer-
ring to all women as Eve, the first woman, who ate the
apple and brought about the Fall. (In a similar metonym-
ous sense, all Jews were identified with the Jews who crucified Christ, and they paid the price for it in many an Easter
pogrom in different parts of Europe. Neither women nor
Jews were clearly seen as individuals.)

As Christ had become "the second Adam," however,
redeeming the catastrophe of the Fall, so the Virgin Mary,
by accepting the role of bearing the God-man, had become
the second Eve. The outlook, therefore, might have seemed
hopeful for women.

> Because it was a woman
> Who built the house for death
> a shining girl tore it down.
> —HILDEGARD

Yet, illogically, as Tertullian revealed, women were still
treated with suspicion, they were still expected to be "silent in the churches," and they were still subject to rigid
"protection" either by father or husband or in enclosure
in a convent. The Virgin Mary had not, after all, lifted
women's status.

Almost all of the women writers—Hadewijch is possibly the sole exception—feel a need in their writings to tell us of their female unworthiness and inferiority. Some of the inferiority, not surprisingly among mystics, has to do with a sense of human unworthiness in relation to God. When Hildegard, for instance, in a shattering vision of what she calls "the Living Light," speaks of herself as "fragile human, ashes of ashes, filth of filth," she may be speaking less of socially conditioned gender perception than of her struggle to take in the difference of scale between God and humanity. A male mystic might easily have said the same thing.

But the women show a more general tendency to denigrate themselves. They are frail, worthless, ignorant, "a weak and fragile rib" (Hildegard); "a useless handmaid and unworthy servant" (Clare); "this creature" (Margery Kempe); "a wretched worm," "a woman ignorant, weak, and frail" (Julian); and their insistence suggests that they are suffering, not surprisingly, from a damaged or broken self-esteem and a socially imposed sense of inferiority, one that the most gifted and talented reveal as much as the least. Some of the self-denigration, I suppose, may have been a literary device, as if the women knew that it was only by abasing themselves that they stood a chance of being listened to, but it is painful to observe women of genius such as Julian or Catherine, or the polymath Hildegard, making their ritual obeisance.

The most striking example comes from the pen of Héloïse, not a mystic but a woman who, having lost her lover Abelard, went on to be a notable religious; she helped to make important reforms in the life of her own Benedictine community in the recognition that Benedict's Rule was not designed with women in mind and did not, in its original form, entirely suit them or their lives. She was originating in France ideas very similar to those Clare was to introduce in Italy fifty years later.

Héloïse was intelligent and superbly educated, and her letters give the reader an oddly modern sense of her ideas. Because of her love for the philosopher Abelard, she was ready to step out of the norms and conventions with extraordinary élan; in her contempt for marriage she puts forward arguments very similar to the ones Simone de Beauvoir would rehearse about her relationship to the philosopher Jean-Paul Sartre centuries later. Urged by Abelard to regularize their relationship by marriage, she had tried to argue him out of it, telling him, as he says, "that only love freely given should keep me for her, not the constriction of a marriage tie."[7]

It is all the more a shock, therefore, to read in one of the letters Héloïse wrote to Abelard, ten years after the catastrophe of his mutilation, her statement that it is the "lot of women to bring total ruin to great men." She quotes Proverbs that woman "has wounded and laid low so many, and the strongest have all been her victims. Her house is the way to hell" and Ecclesiastes, "I find woman more bitter than death; she is a snare, her heart a net, her arms are chains." And she goes on to rehearse the Genesis story. "It was the first woman in the beginning who lured man from Paradise, and she who had been created by the Lord as his helpmate became the instrument of his total downfall."[8] No doubt she suffered great guilt about Abelard's downfall, yet it is tragic the way she immediately assumes the role of Eve, as if Abelard, a mature man at the time he met her, a mere schoolgirl, had no responsibility for his own actions. It is clear from Abelard's own words in the account he wrote of himself known as *Historia Calamitatum* that he had cold-bloodedly decided to seduce a woman, and after considering the possibilities, he picked on Héloïse, partly because of the convenience of being left alone with her in his role as teacher. In her need to blame herself entirely for the outcome, she showed herself a woman of her time.

Painfully as women suffered, however, from the misogynist prejudice that had crept into Christianity, they found their own ways of taking heart and surviving. They took comfort, for example, in the flawless femininity of the Virgin Mary herself, as many of their poems testify. She may not have elevated women very successfully, but nevertheless, through her all women had been touched, or rather had known themselves to be inhabited by, divinity.

> O wonder!
> To a submissive
> woman
> the king came bowing. . . .
> "But malice flowed from woman?"
> So from woman felicity
> overflows. . . .
> [She] brings more grace to heaven
> than ever disgrace to earth.
>
> —HILDEGARD

A sense of fellow feeling for the Virgin—the only female role model available to these women—gave them a remarkable sense of intimacy with her. Margery Kempe, always one for the literal approach, sees herself in her meditations bustling about in the household of the Holy

Family, helping to bath Jesus and wrap him in his swaddling clothes.

The women mystics love and revere Mary (some much more than others, Julian perhaps showing the least interest) but also draw strength and encouragement from this powerful and beautiful female image. The image of the baby in its mother's arms, on her lap, sucking at her breast, recapitulates a universal human experience and is one of the most dominant of archetypes, as generations of artists have shown. This profound yet popular image has been of incalculable importance to Christian awareness.

The Virgin Mary was relayed to women as a model of quiet femininity—obedient, submissive, and as it was inferred, rightly or wrongly, from the gospels, largely silent, content to exist not primarily as her own person but only in relation to her son. But the reverence male clerics felt for Mary did not seem to make much difference to the way they thought about other women, who were still subjected to a strict surveillance as if at any moment they might repeat the mistake that initiated the Fall.

Few, if any, of the women in this book are "contained," as it were, by the archetype of Mary. Angela and Margery, who both experienced motherhood, never appear to seek to find God in that particular experience, whereas Julian places motherhood not primarily in the Virgin but within the Godhead itself. Angela's spirituality, like that of a number of holy women, takes a much more overtly sexual form, with images of marriage to Christ predominating.

In the period covered by this book, from the twelfth century to the early fifteenth, women are beginning to stretch the boundaries of the confinement forced on the collective Eve, even, in important ways, to break free of it. While loving Mary and drawing some female strength from her gentle motherliness, they are seeking a less passive role for themselves. Many of them—Christina, Hadewijch, Mechthild of Magdeburg, Clare, Angela, Catherine, Marguerite Porete, Margery Kempe—far from being passive, offend actively against the conventions of their society, the authority of their fathers, or the authority of the Church, and in some cases, like that of Christina, against all three. There was a note of subversion common to most women mystics, a subversion not so much of the teenage rebellion type, though there are hints of that here and there, as one resulting from the difficult and painful discovery that their own truth did not allow them to behave like other people, especially other women. They argued and struggled and grieved and prayed as it became ever clearer in the case of each individual that she simply could not fit into the pattern that was prescribed for her.

The pattern was rigid, as it was for all women. The most obvious pattern began with a limited, often purely domestic, education, followed by marriage in the midteens or earlier. Marriage was designed to lead a woman into a "good" and prosperous family—in the case of the well-born, one that might obliquely bring prestige or possessions to the girl's parents, or to a husband with a thriving trade in the case of those lower down the social scale; the marriage would be followed by repeated pregnancies and the births of many children. Childbirth quite frequently resulted in the death of the mother—Catherine, herself the twenty-fourth of twenty-five children, was not unusual in seeing one of her elder sisters die in this way.

Since medieval women were generally seen to be in

need of protection, either from the brutality of the male sexual appetite or from their own wayward nature, the other option endorsed by society was to enter a convent and lead a life of "enclosure," forbidden to leave in any but the gravest circumstances. In either marriage or convent they passed from the control of their fathers to the control of another man, since even in convents, abbesses were increasingly overseen by male clerics. Women must have experienced themselves as male chattels.

Hildegard was a chattel in a different sense. She was a tenth child, and her wealthy parents gave her away as a tithe, to the recluse Jutta, at the tender age of eight. She was to write with bitterness of the wrongness of committing young children to the religious life as oblates, suggesting, acutely, that the parents were forcing the child to a pious service they were not prepared to undertake themselves. "He is neither dead to the world, nor alive in it. And why have you oppressed him to such an extent that he is capable of neither?" (*Scivias*). Nothing irrevocable in the way of vows should be permitted, she says, until the child is old enough to give consent. It speaks volumes of her own sense of betrayal as a child.

The sample of women discussed and illustrated in this book all contrived to subvert the prescribed pattern of women's lives, consciously or, far more probably, unconsciously, insisting on (to use an anachronistic word) "control." To a considerable degree they achieved it: control of the way they lived their lives; control of the world around them by the observations they made on it, in speech or writing; control, in a number of cases—Hildegard, Clare, the Beguines—of the way communities of women were to structure their lives, independently of male theories on the subject.

The most striking innovators were the Beguines, who originated in northern Europe. No one is quite sure of the source of their name—perhaps the most charming version is that they are named after Lambert le Bègue, Lambert the Stammerer, who founded both them and their male counterpart, the Beghards. Both were an inspired new form of Christianity that recalled some features of the apostles in Acts, most notably, perhaps, the use of people's homes as centers of Christian living but also the informality and equality of the communities. They managed to be both active and contemplative, living in simplicity, going about caring for lepers and for the poor and the sick, but embracing a life of prayer. They were essentially a lay movement. For the Beghards it was new enough, but for the women—unmarried women or widows—it represented a radical freedom.

Living, some in their own homes, some sharing with fellow Beguines, some, as the movement grew, in Beguinages—groups of houses, even small villages, given over to Beguines—they were more or less self-supporting. The way of life allowed a good deal of individuality—some were simply contemplatives—but it also encouraged sisterhood, a sharing of skills such as reading and writing, works of charity undertaken together, and it was based on an equality of members rather than the rigid hierarchy of the Benedictine convent.

Some women mystics—Hildegard, Clare, the Helfta women—chose the convent, but most of them saw the need for changing the *forma vitae* in order to impose distinctly female characteristics on it. Clare was disappointed that it was not thought possible for the Poor Ladies, or Poor Clares, the female counterpart of the Franciscan friars, to lead the wandering life of their brothers, caring for the poor and the sick. It seems that this was what Francis had at first had in mind for the women led by Clare, but that convention and propriety had defeated the intention. Hildegard broke with the abbot of Disibodenberg, to his considerable fury, to set up first one, then another, convent away from his jurisdiction. Clare instituted radical reforms (most notably reducing the severity of enclosure and insisting that women had the stamina to endure poverty as well as men). The Helfta Cistercians and, in a different way, the Beguines designed a sisterhood shaped around love and learning. Each, in their own way, distanced their enterprise from male jurisdiction, though Clare used her patron, Francis, to lend validity to her reform.

Angela, Catherine, and Margery found unique vocations for themselves. Angela, a Third Order Franciscan, went about doing good works and caring for the sick in the way that Clare would have liked to have done a century before. Catherine of Siena worked among plague victims and became noted as a religious teacher, the heart and soul of a group of reformers; this led her toward political involvement on behalf of the church. Margery became a tremendous traveler, a sort of perpetual pilgrim. Apart from setting up two convents and being a writer and scientist and composer, Hildegard preached in public, traveling widely around Germany in order to do so. Julian, while leading the life of enclosure as an anchoress and not obviously flouting male authority, managed somehow to be the most subversive of all. Maybe for her, as for Christina, the life of a recluse, by its hiddenness, granted a necessary freedom from external interference.

Convents, though rigidly enclosed, offered certain advantages, giving an alternative for women who did not wish for marriage or childbearing. That was not all they offered. "Until the fourteenth century," says Elizabeth Petroff, "a religious community was the only place a woman could find the opportunity to read and write, along with a library of books and other scholars to talk to; it was also the only place a woman had any privacy, where she could be expected to be alone with her thoughts."[9] The convent could also act as protection if questions were asked about the orthodoxy of a particular member—ecclesiastical authority feared to challenge influential orders, and all the big orders had powerful friends in high places who might put in a word for them in season. A possible illustration of this function of the convent is when Mechthild, who admits herself frightened about getting into trouble for her writing, joins the Cistercian community at Helfta in her old age after a lifetime as a Beguine. Hadewijch became somehow disgraced in her Beguine life, maybe as a result of external disapproval, although it appears that she was driven out of her leadership position by the Beguines themselves.

The problems arose for women of strong character and original opinions living in societies where they were permitted little self-expression. With or without enclosure, virginity was felt by them to be a key to the freedom they needed, much as it seemed to the young women in the Carthaginian church. It was generally felt to be a better and nobler state than marriage, so that women who received little respect as a rule could obtain it by being vowed to a life of virginity. Again there was the hope of its removing the taint of Eve, or perhaps even in a metaphorical sense making a woman genderless, since she was sexually unavailable. Medieval people tended to believe that women were by nature sexually voracious, much more so than men, so that for women to renounce sexual expression seemed all the more remarkable. The practical advantage of the sacrifice was that they were not subject to a husband or weakened and preoccupied by repeated pregnancies and child care. Virginity was a bid for freedom, in the sense common to both women and men that Peter Brown described in the early church—a radical overcoming of nature; for women it was also a device for making it easier to take control of their own lives, an argument used by some suffragettes much later in history.

It is, however, impossible to read what medieval people wrote about virginity without finding oneself in a mindset difficult for a twentieth-century person to understand. "Nor do I think that virgins only will be saved," says Christina, in an argument with the prior of Saint Albans, Fredebertus, "but I say . . . and it is true, that if many virgins perish, so rather do married women. And if many mothers of families are saved . . . certainly virgins are saved more easily." The contempt for marriage and for sexuality, the conviction that virginity was the only suitable path to spiritual growth, all suggest what medieval people did indeed believe, that the human condition is innately deplorable (part of "the shipwreck of this world," as Hildegard calls it) and only by shedding most natural human appetites is God to be apprehended. It is puzzling that they do not care to consider that God gave them their appetites, that without them they could not long survive as individuals, and that without sexuality the human race would quickly die out. For them the journey toward holiness involves a bitter and protracted struggle with all the appetites—eating, drinking, and sleeping as well as the sexual instinct, as if duality is fighting it out in their very being.

Spiritual enlightenment apart, it is fascinating to see these women coping with the unusual experience of power—and almost all of them were leaders and/or counselors.

On one level they were, and distinctly knew themselves to be, frail instruments through whom God was making himself known, in itself a frightening, as well as marvelous, knowledge. But, intoxicating for silent daughters of Eve, they were also noticed, they were seen and heard. Whether it is also true that the sort of people who became holy women (and men) had a special and particular need to be seen as singular, to possess this ambivalent form of power, I am not sure. It would not be surprising, but I do not see that this need, if it is that, detracts from their holiness. It could be seen as one important and useful strand in their vocation.

I admire their ability to "show off," as people must have said at the time, to make sure that they were noticed, even though this was a risky business. I admire their courage and their subversiveness, and in particular I admire their ability to get their own way.

The cost of becoming visible and audible, of taking a path with no role model walking ahead, was considerable, and the women paid for it, and for the physical effect of shattering psychic experiences, with severe and disabling illnesses that frequently prostrated them for long periods;

the various extreme forms of austerity widely practiced among them must also have contributed to their poor health, of course.

Hildegard suffered from illness of a migrainous type for most of her life, often being unable to move for days at a time, which suggests that she was deeply conflicted. Since the day of her birth, she tells us, speaking of herself in the third person, she was "troubled by continual pain in all her veins, marrow and flesh. . . . Frequently she is affected by great fatigue. Sometimes she is affected quite mildly; at other times, more seriously, when she is brought to exhaustion by her illness" (Scivias). Everything affects her condition—"the air itself, from the rain, from the wind, from every sort of weather." But, psychologically aware, she notes that it is through this disabling experience that she is the person she is, that she can perceive, as she puts it, "some of the mysteries of God." Illness, and the questioning and time for reflection it has produced, have helped to form the mature Hildegard.

Clare was bedridden for much of her long adult life. (Perhaps she resented the sacrifices of her life more than she could admit to.) Mechthild wrote, "For twenty years I was never but tired, ill and weak." Julian's visions began in an illness in which she hung between life and death. Catherine was a considerable invalid and died, at thirty-three, from simply giving up food (a fascinating parallel here with Simone Weil). The exercise of power was, for such women, we might suppose, full of conflict caused by emotions that they found it unseemly to admit to, and later holy women—Teresa of Ávila, Thérèse of Lisieux, Bernadette—confirm this impression.

Severe penances were perhaps another way in which

they dealt with severe inner conflict. Male mystics also practiced penances, but it is generally agreed that the women were much more extreme, perhaps in part because of the belief in feminine weakness or spiritual frailty.

"Deliberate and systematic physical punishment was part of the daily routine for many religious women," says Caroline Walker Bynum.

> Alda of Siena, for example . . . slept on a bed of paving stones, whipped herself with chains, wore a crown of thorns, and carved for herself, as an object of devotion, a wooden nail like the one that pierced Christ's feet. Dorothy of Montau put herself through a pantomime of the Crucifixion that involved praying with her arms in the form of a cross and later, in imitation of Christ's burial, lying prostrate with the entire weight of her body supported only by toes, nose and forehead. Jane Mary of Maille stuck a thorn into her head in remembrance of Christ's crown of thorns. Reading the lives of fourteenth- and fifteenth-century women greatly expands one's knowledge of Latin synonyms for whip, thong, flail, chain, etc. Ascetic practices commonly reported in these *vitae* include wearing hair shirts, binding the flesh tightly with twisted ropes, rubbing lice into self-inflicted wounds, denying oneself sleep, adulterating food and water with ashes or salt, performing thousands of genuflections, thrusting nettles into one's breasts, and praying barefoot in winter. Among the more bizarre female behaviors were rolling in broken glass, jumping into ovens, hanging from a gibbet, and praying upside down.[10]

She quotes a description of sisters, during Advent and Lent, "hacking at themselves" cruelly with whips, in the chapter house after matins, until the blood flowed. (It is impossible to read this without wondering how they managed not to die of blood poisoning, gangrene, burns, pneumonia, or other serious illnesses brought on by maltreating the body. Perhaps some of them did.)

"There is no question that the experiencing of pain was a prominent aspect of the spirituality of both late medieval women and late medieval men. There is no question that it was more prominent in women's religiosity."[11]

While men might practice some fairly extreme forms of penance themselves, one feature, according to Caroline Bynum, was almost exclusively female. This was a psychosomatic imitation of the sufferings of Christ, with the wounds of Christ's body during the Crucifixion—the marks of scourges and nails—appearing on women's bodies. They often bled on Fridays, or at the hour of the Crucifixion. Women also sometimes showed what were known as espousal rings, marks on the wedding finger that indicated their intimate relationship to Christ.

Identification with the agony of Christ was a very powerful form of spirituality throughout late medieval times, as devotion to Christ triumphant changed to a devotion to the suffering Christ, but the women seem to pass beyond imaginative imitation to a state of fusion. Flowing blood, Bynum says, plays an important part both in their lives (in their penances) and in their visions.

Angela, after her visions, "was able to participate in the Crucifixion with her own body."[12] An important stage in her conversion, one in which perhaps she was imitating the gesture of Saint Francis when he stripped himself naked, was to tear off her clothes as she stood before a crucifix of the naked Christ in the Church of Saint Francis. She felt that "the Cross entered her body." Among many severe forms of penance, Angela drank the liquid in which she had washed the sores of lepers. (Lepers, like the poor, were seen by the followers of Francis as "alter Christus.")

Catherine received the stigmata, the ultimate fusion, but Julian's identification with Christ does not take the crudely literal form of reproducing the signs of crucifixion on her own body. While wishing passionately that she had been present among the women at the Crucifixion, she thinks more symbolically, recognizing that what is asked of her is an inner growth and identification. Recalling the three wounds on her neck suffered by Saint Cecilia in her martyrdom, Julian asks, "in the course of my life," for three wounds of her own, all of an "inner" kind: the wound of contrition, the wound of compassion, and the wound of longing for God.

Both Caroline Bynum and Elizabeth Petroff see medieval women as defined, and confined, by their bodies. "Women were bodies [men were characterized as mind or spirit], and bodies were dangerous—dangerous to men and therefore dangerous to society as a whole. The physical austerities undergone by women mystics, and that young women often imposed on themselves, underscored society's need to control and purify the female body."[13]

Another of these methods was extremely severe fasting, shown in its most extraordinary form in Catherine of Siena, who fasted to the point that she could no longer eat and had the sense that if she did eat it would be a form of suicide; in fact she died, at thirty-three, of not eating. Some degree of extreme refusal of food was practiced by many medieval religious women and was a source of great fascination to contemporaries. Fasting was, of course, a common religious practice, but that some of these women lived for long periods without eating at all, or stopped excreting or urinating, seemed miraculous.

Bynum warns against too glib a modern diagnosis of these conditions as anorexia nervosa or bulimia, even though so many features—abstention from food, intense interest in the idea of food, vomiting after taking food, misapprehensions of the body itself—are so similar; the cultures, she says, are so very different, and therefore the constructs on women abstaining from food must be different too. Medieval women were not concerned, as women are today, with an ideal thinness, something often thought to be the explanation of anorexia among contemporary young women. She suggests that medieval people were not as naive as we may suppose about human conduct, and that they already understood the idea of pathological abstention from food. (In fact Angela, in one of her ecstasies, sees "not to eat or to eat only very little" as a temptation). But Bynum points out that another modern idea about anorexia—the need for a sense of control by someone, often an adolescent girl, who feels deprived of it—is very relevant to medieval women, and I have already suggested that control may have been an important motivation for the women in this book. Anorexia was, for them, as for their modern counterparts, a way of manipulating people from a position experienced as weak.

Bynum seeks to dismiss masochism as a serious motive behind the penances and anorexia of the women mystics, and I wonder if she is right about this, since, in its origins, masochism so often seems to be the psychological resource of those who feel weak (children, for example) and who are painfully stressed by the power of others. Helplessness, shame, and obscure guilt become bearable through identifying with powerful persons and being in submission to them (therefore, in a sense, sharing in their power); it is a sort of "best of a bad job" in an intolerable situation. This seems a likely device for women in medieval (and many other) times, and perhaps the quality of helplessness and woundedness in the Crucifixion itself strengthened its appeal for women, suggesting that their own unwanted condition was written into the very fabric of human existence, though the redeeming quality of Jesus is that he does not identify with the brute evil that destroys him, and is therefore not, in fact, masochistic.

Penance and starvation apart, some of the women reveal masochistic traits in their writing. A number of them used a religious version of the romance, a literary form which itself contained masochistic strains in its exploration of unrequited or unconsummated love, so making it easier for its imitators to reveal this strain in their own feelings. Quoting Marguerite Porete's description in *The Mirror of Simple Souls* of her immense joy in the divine lover, Peter Dronke goes on to describe the torment which, for her, accompanies such love: "[She] imagines a series of tests in which her lover treats her with callous cruelty to gauge how complete is her amorous submission to him. It is only after extravagant unconditional surrender to each of his cruelties that the soul imagines him giving her an unconditional reward. . . . The fantasies of heartless deception go beyond any comparable motifs known . . . in the world of profane romances."[14] Marguerite's lover tortures her by asking what she would do if he ordered her to love another rather than himself, or, alternatively, if he preferred another to her. All of these fantasies of power can be found in sadomasochistic literature, in fact the modern

*Story of O* is almost identical in the hero's abuse of the female character.

For love of Francis Clare had left a prosperous and indulged life to live in poverty, and enclosure, and he remained in a platonic sense her lover, the one through whom she saw the vision of God. In the *Fioretti* there is an account of her repeated request to Francis to be allowed to eat with him, something she had apparently never done. His fellow friars tell him roundly that they think he is 'too severe' with her in refusing such a modest request—'above all, when we consider that through thy preaching she forsook the "pomps and riches of this world."' Rather grudgingly Francis appears to agree, invites Clare and a sister to the Portiuncula, having given her special permission to leave the convent of San Damiano, where she "hath for long been shut up." In fact, when Clare arrives and sits on the ground with Francis to eat supper, Francis begins to preach in such a way that "corporeal food" is forgotten. Perhaps it was a marvelous occasion and not in any sense a disappointment, but Clare's wish to eat with him seems simple and natural enough to have been granted, as plainly the brothers thought it should have been. Worse, when Francis is near to death, Clare, who this time has no permission to leave San Damiano, sends an urgent message that she wants to see him. Francis promises her that she will, and then gives an instruction that after he is dead the brothers are to carry his corpse down to San Damiano and hold it up at the window, so that, in a sense, Clare will "see him again."

No doubt Francis wished to point to truths that lay deeper than human affections, but there is an element of sinister joke in these stories that has perhaps less to do with holy humor than with unconscious cruelty.

The abuse of power, and the readiness of Marguerite or Clare to submit to it, is shocking unless, and I find this an interesting idea, it is possible to imagine that within the love of God even perverted forms of love are reflected and redeemed.

The kind of reticence that exists in hagiographical writing has sometimes inhibited those who wrote about holy men and women from confronting the neurotic aspects of their subjects, perhaps from a fear that this might make their holiness less believable or valuable. In fact, some writers fall over backward to assert that the most bizarre kinds of human behavior, the sort that, if presented to us in our daily lives, would have us telephoning the police or the psychiatrist, are nothing of the kind if the person involved is prestigious and holy enough.

I wonder if this does justice to the complexity of human beings and the peculiar ways in which certain kinds of truth become known to us. The people we are studying are visionaries, women with the most extraordinary and detailed awareness of things that most of us never catch a glimpse of—God on his throne, the Holy Spirit, Jesus on the cross, the Virgin Mary, heaven, hell, angels, the nature of love, the nature of evil. The huge events happening in their minds have repercussions in their bodies, making them unable to eat, filling them (in some cases) with sexual sensations, causing them to weep or scream, to reveal "espousal rings" on their wedding fingers or the stigmata on their bodies, and very, very frequently, inflicting bouts of severe illness on them. These are not normal ways of living, and mystics are not normal people. If we try too hard either to pretend they are "like us" or to ignore the fact that their behavior strikes us as very peculiar indeed, it becomes even more difficult to get past the blocks to whatever is good and original and interesting in what they have to say. Their lives turn into chaos.

At times the women seem unbearably stressed by the demands of the seismic inner event, as if it cracks asunder the simple humanness of convention and ordinary awareness and opens into a madness that in turn opens into a different sanity. But the human vessel is broken by the power that rushes through it, and it seems to be this possibility of destruction to which these women have given a sometimes reluctant assent.

Just as pictures of the martyrs depict their wounds or the instruments of their suffering (Saint Catherine of Alexandria with her wheel, Sebastian with his arrows) as if to show that even in a glorified state the injuries themselves are still integral to the person, so it may be that through wounds in the psyche, cracks in the personality, neurotic or psychotic traits, through depression and hysteria and paranoia, a way is made for the transcendent to reach into the human condition. As a much later hymn writer, a Protestant, was to suggest:

> The shines of heaven rush sweetly in
> At all the gaping flaws;
> Visions of endless bliss are seen,
> And native air she draws.[15]

The injuries become the doorway into knowledge. Like artists, who are notorious for not being "normal," not "fitting in," saints are tormented, and delighted, by a visitation that reaches them in ways not in the least conventional. They are stretched, sometimes beyond their bearing, by a perception so oblique and unusual that it may strike dread into those who hear it.

The visions come to the women in various ways and are by no means identical. For some of them the vision is more a way of life, perceived early, in childhood or teens, that obsesses them so entirely that they hold to it through every kind of disapproval and setback.

For Hildegard there were extraordinary movements of light around people and objects from earliest childhood. This play of light had profound spiritual significance for her, though it was linked to an unbearably distressing form of migraine. Her visions, as described by her in the *Scivias,* are composed of portentous symbols—mountains and precious stones and serried ranks of angels—reminiscent of the Book of Ezekiel or the Book of Revelation. They seem oddly "improving," as she comes back from the divine throne with messages that are a bit of an anticlimax. She tells us whether priests may marry twice, whether women may be ordained (they may not), whether people suffer eternal torment if they are not baptized (they do), whether deformed children are made that way as a reproof to their parents (they are), whether men should touch their genitals (they should not).

It is disappointing to discover that God had nothing new to say on these and other questions and impossible not to believe that the visions say at least as much about the prejudices Hildegard carried into them as about any new revelation. In fact it may be that *Scivias* is simply a literary form using vision, or pseudovision, as a teaching device.

Certainly *Scivias* seems less about communion with

God (Hildegard shows no interest in the Unitive Way) than about a rather heavy pedagogy. Hildegard is more exegete, preacher, and teacher than visionary, and a rather prim and proper one at that, lecturing her audience on knowing their place and behaving properly. Women, especially, should know their place, "for they are an infirm and weak habitation, appointed to bear children and diligently nurture them."

Happily, however, her poetry shows an entirely different and much more attractive side of Hildegard, the passion of an ardent mind richly endowed.

Hildegard enjoyed acceptance from the clerical world of her day, and although she is critical of "the world," and even, rather bravely, of the emperor, Frederick Barbarossa, an erstwhile champion of hers, she sides strongly with orthodoxy. At clerical suggestion, she wrote a condemnation of the Cathars.

Clare has almost nothing to say of her ecstasies, though in her letters there is a sense of rapture that suggests that the joy and meaning she felt as a girl when she first heard Francis preach in Assisi has remained with her. The upside-down world of Francis in which poverty is riches, and death life, still excites and inspires her.

Angela's visionary life was a kind of spiral, sweeping her upward as she meditated on the truths of Christianity, until the day when she offers "her whole self" to Christ. Next comes a desire for poverty and a giving away of her possessions, and then a number of appearances of Jesus to her, on the cross. Sometimes these occur in dreams, sometimes when she is in a waking state. She has a vision of the heart of Christ, accompanied by the words "In this heart, there is no falsehood, but only truth." This is followed by a vision of the blood flowing freely from Christ's side, and Angela puts her mouth to the wound and drinks from it.

In alternating ecstasies and agonies, Angela moved into an ever more comprehensive vision of God. There were bouts of screaming, of physical collapse, and of sweetness so unbearable that she wanted to die.

Later, after a pilgrimage to Assisi, Angela heard the words of Jesus promising her betrothal to him. Later again she heard a voice saying "You are full of God." Her whole experience is extraordinarily personal, as if the point and meaning of it is the intensity of her relationship with God and the transformations it produces in her.

In this she is unlike Julian, with her persistent Job-like questions about the meaning of suffering, her concern about whether some souls are damned. Julian's vision, reproduced in full in the short text here, has none of the sexual overtones of Angela's experience, no trace of the *Brautmystik*—the bridal imagery used by many women mystics. Julian's need seems less emotional, less concerned with feeling herself loved (though she does feel this) than with being allowed to *know*.

Yet her writing shines with an extraordinary tenderness and love—she describes God as "our clothing, for he is that love which wraps and enfolds us, embraces us and guides us, surrounds us with his love, which is so tender that he may never desert us" (Short text). Her later idea of God as mother (as well as father) develops the intimacy of this thought. God as mother was a fairly common medieval idea, but Julian's elaboration of it seems like a sudden extension of understanding, a vast reworking of the Trinity; it is also a celebration, perhaps rare at the time, of the marvelous power of women to carry new life and give it birth. Suddenly the feminine becomes precious and admirable, not simply because of the Virgin Mary (Julian is less interested in the Virgin than many medieval writers) but because she sees it to be good and beautiful in itself, and it has become for her a window into the wonder of God. Julian's statements about the motherhood of God are therefore "feminist" statements in the most direct sense of the word. Along with this goes a sense of the tranquillity of resting in God—"God is rest," she says.

Margery Kempe's visions are inextricable from the details of her life—she lives in a state of constant commerce with God, frequently discussing her condition, and the inexplicable hostility of others, with Jesus. He gives her reassuring replies. There is a quality of a clown about Margery, both in comic and tragic aspects—her spiritual life is conducted not merely in the vernacular but in an earthy and literal vein that foreshadows the speeches of Shakespeare's "mechanicals." Margery is very given to tears, noisy and intrusive ones that interrupt church services and tend to irritate well-behaved people. There is something attention seeking about them (as also about the rather smug way she tells about them), yet they also indicate a level of suffering in Margery, caught as she is between the expectations of a woman in her world—expectations that have brought her fourteen pregnancies and a husband who continues to demand his "conjugal rights"—and her own intense spiritual longings. Yet "many times when [she] was in church our Lord Jesus Christ with his glorious mother, and many saints as well, came into her soul. . . . And she also heard many times a voice of a sweet bird singing in her ear, and often she heard sweet sounds and melodies that surpassed her wit to tell of them" (*The Book of Margery Kempe*).

What, we may wonder, does the writing of these women give us as readers? Apart from a literary interest and the fascination of studying such early expressions of women's thoughts, what religious or theological residue remains? All of them wrote at the time of the great human love affair or marriage with Christianity, in which almost all art and thought existed in relation to it and the passion it inspired. We live in a colder spiritual climate from which much of that passion has faded, and we have the difficult task of deciding whether to separate ourselves from that significant phase of the human past or to reinterpret Christianity afresh.

Theologically the majority of the women seem innovative, not so much because of the originality of their thought as because of the strangeness of their situation as women trying to speak to the needs of their time. Just as Francis recognized that in lepers and beggars there was a vision of Christ to be discovered, so medieval women, with their parallel experience of powerlessness, shadowed forth a lost wisdom that a triumphant Church had mislaid.

From our perspective maybe the Beguines made the most original and interesting contribution as they worked out their theology of love unpretentiously in the Bequinages of the Low Countries. They were seeking a female autonomy within which to lead a more authentic Christian life, and there was a naturalness about their lives relative to the more extreme and structured forms of religion around them that seemed to tap back and down into the simplicity and naturalness of the life Christ led with his disciples. The Beguines are relevant to contemporary women, on the fringes of the church or right outside it, who are yet interested in exploring Christian spiritual ideas, and also in the creative discovery of sisterhood. But the importance stretches beyond women's needs. Lay communities, whether formal or informal, with men and women living together or separately, now seem likely to be one of the ways that Christian ideas will be carried on to future generations.

Clare's vision, very much within the monastic tradition, although full of the vitality of the Franciscan life, is modest in that it does not seek to preach or reform outside her own very specific experience, yet it is perfect like a jewel. Clare set up a network of earthly communities, San Damiano and its sister houses, each trying to realize the Incarnation and "the kingdom" right where they were in their life of poverty and love with one another—"joy of heaven to earth come down." Every line of Clare's *forma vitae*, with its unhierarchical, humane, thoughtful vision of a community proclaims the idea of love that she had caught from Francis, yet seems so naturally her own.

Angela's vision, like Hildegard's, is conformist and unsurprising in its theology—no cardinal's blood pressure would rise while reading her book—yet she brings to her spiritual exploration an extraordinary quality of religious joy that modifies, for a modern reader, the strange and repulsive strands of her experience.

The joy of the Beguine writers, like Angela's, is full of sexual undertones—the Beguines play their hide-and-seek with the divine lover, torn between excitement, joy, and fear.

Catherine is concerned, like Hildegard, with a didactic task; she is supremely a teacher and is acknowledged as

such by the church, the only woman apart from Teresa of
Ávila to be called doctor. Her teaching role, coupled with
her reformist zeal, is much in evidence in her *Dialogue.*
The book has a rather minatory note of dressings-down
and "putting people in their place," something the late
medieval church doubtless deserved. Her slightly bullying
tone reminded me of those formidable women apostles of
temperance in the late nineteenth and early twentieth centuries. Their motives were unexceptionable—drink caused
a lot of human misery—but nevertheless they were annoy-
ingly self-righteous, and it is difficult not to feel that the
energy and passion they put into the cause had got displaced from other areas of their lives. Catherine is very
taken up with the devil, with wickedness and sin. Yet she
is also bound on the Unitive Way. Through virtue, self-
knowledge, and "humble prayer," she describes the soul
drawing nearer to God. "Following in the footsteps of
Christ crucified, and through desire and affection and the
union of love, he makes of her another himself. So Christ
seems to have meant when he said, 'If you will love me
and keep my word, I will show myself to you, and you will
be one thing with me and I with you'" (*Dialogue*). The
purpose at the heart of Christianity has perhaps never been
better put outside the Gospels.

Of all these women, Julian is the most theologically
minded, the most daring, perhaps the least concerned with
the problem of being a woman. She loves God with a naturalness and ease and a simple security, yet she pushes beyond received ideas to ask questions that have deeply
troubled her in the lonely life of the cell and no doubt have
often emerged as she has acted as counselor to troubled
people in the community in which she lives. Why does God

allow suffering and evil in the world? Are souls damned for eternity? Suffering, evil, damnation, are realized by her in her "Showings," as is the crucifixion event that stands at the heart of the conundrum. She wants to understand whatever a loving human being can understand, to see how the gap between God and poor fallible human beings can be bridged, how the duality between eternity and time can become a unity. And her reply comes like Job's in terms of a change of perspective as she sees the "at-one-ing" of the Crucifixion and when she sees "all that is made" as tiny as a hazelnut compared with the greatness of God. But for her, unlike Job, there is an extraordinary sense of the tenderness of God, a motherliness caught up and expressed within the Trinity itself. "As truly as God is our Father, so truly is God our Mother, and he revealed that in everything, and especially in these sweet words where he says: I am he; that is to say: I am he, the power and goodness of fatherhood; I am he, the wisdom and the lovingness of motherhood; I am he, the light and the grace which is all blessed love; I am he, the Trinity; I am he, the unity; I am he, the great supreme goodness of every kind of thing; I am he who makes you to love; I am he who makes you to long: I am he, the endless fulfilling of all true desires" (Long text). While opening herself to the supreme heights and depths of the Revelations or Showings, Julian is at all times balanced by a counterweight of sanity and common sense that makes her emerge to the reader as entirely trustworthy. She seems to have little sense of personal need—for reassurance, for attention, for the satisfactions associated with a lover. The whole Unitive experience is, for her, suffused with love. It reminds her in its self-giving of the generosity of the feeding mother.

While Julian seems to me to be as profound, as moving, as boldly innovative as any mystic I can think of, with insights that have still to be integrated into Christian thinking, I was also delighted by a tiny fragment of the writing of Marguerite Porete, which feels oddly modern in its understanding. Following her highly erotic understanding of the Unitive Way, Marguerite tells a story of a kind of remote "falling in love," with which it is perfectly possible to empathize today; in fact many of us have had similar experiences.

> Once upon a time there was a maiden, a king's daughter, of great heart and gentleness, and of fine spirit too; she lived in a foreign land. It came to pass that she heard tell of the great courtliness and nobility of King Alexander, and at once in intent she loved him, because of the great renown of his noble excellence. Yet this maiden was so far from the great lord in whom she had spontaneously set her love, she could neither see him nor possess him. Because of this she was often disconsolate within herself, since no love save this contented her. And when she saw that this far-off love, which was so close to her, or inside her, was so far outside, she thought she would solace her unease by somehow imagining the looks of her friend, for whose sake she was so often rent in heart. Then she had an image painted, which portrayed the semblance of the king she loved, as close as she could get to portraying the way she loved him, in the affection of the love that held her; and by means of this image, together with her other practices, she dreamt the king himself.[16]

This little story, intending to suggest that it is possible to love God while feeling distanced from him, somehow in spite of itself suggests an alternative—that God may be, at least in part, our own invention. The mystics, or perhaps all who believe in God, may be guilty of huge projections. This problem is not peculiar to the relationship with God, of course. Many human relationships can prove to be illusory, not in the sense that another person does not exist but because the lover misreads the beloved by projecting his or her own needs and may, in fact, be in love with a largely fictional character, much as the princess was in love with Alexander.

Yet maybe part of the point of loving God, or other people, is to pass beyond personal needs to a true perception of the other—maybe that *is* the discipline that love, whether divine or human, imposes. If this is the way toward reality, then it is one that involves austerities and penances of its own.

But we have not yet come to the difficult nub in understanding the mystical experience of the women in this book, of the saints who followed them, and of many unsung women in history. All of the women quoted here either had never experienced sexual intercourse or, like Margery and Angela, felt that the fact that they had experienced it was regrettable, a contamination. Occasionally desire revisited the two who had known married love, but it was a temptation of the devil to be fiercely resisted, having no part in their new, spiritual lives. Héloïse alone, unusual in this as in so many ways, reports her sexual longings without shame or even, I think, regret. Such regret as she has is for the loss of the man she loved and still longs for and, even more strongly, for the harm her association has done to her lover. For Héloïse sexual desire is quite distinct from what she feels about God. But Héloïse, unlike the others, is not a mystic.

For most of the other women this is not so. For Hadewijch, Beatrijs, Mechtild, Angela, Catherine, fantasies of approach and withdrawal, even of cruelty and submission, are part of their prayer life, part of the extraordinary drama of the soul in its relation to God. Only Julian, whose relationship seems to be of a different kind, and Hildegard, whose relation to Richardis von Stade does at least raise the possibility that her sexual desire may have been more toward women than men, seems not to feel the powerful pull of male/female desire in her encounter with God.

So, are we to conclude that what we are looking at in these women is a displacement of sexual desire—a removal of it from the more ordinary object of lover and husband and a projection of it onto God? The scholar of mysticism, Evelyn Underhill, deplored the reductionist attitude to the ecstatic experience of saints that suggests that it is "only" a sign of sexual repression. Yet if human desire was somehow displaced by the mystics onto God, would it matter?

Reading the women mystics, I find myself catching a glimpse of something that goes beyond "women's experience" or neurosis or sexual repression or hysteria or any of the labels with which we push away what is strange and hard to bear. Whatever their blind spots, their dualistic understanding of sexuality, they seem to know something important. Looking out through the cracks of their human prisons, what these women find is an indescribable beauty and joy and wonder. The "everyday" sense of time and place is swallowed up in an entirely new perspective, an extraordinary awareness of pattern and power and glory and love. We are privileged to use their eyes, their descriptions, their visions, as human beings for centuries used the journals of intrepid travelers to learn about what they dare not go and see for themselves.

They suggest that beyond the endemic human conflict between sexuality and spirituality there is a unity and a healing scarcely to be guessed at.

Mechthild says:

> It is a rare
> And a high way,
> Which the soul follows,
> Drawing the senses after.

NOTES

1. Saint-Martin, quoted by Evelyn Underhill in the preface to *Mysticism* (London Methuen, 1911), xiii.

2. Elizabeth A. Petroff, preface to *Body and Soul: Essays on Medieval Women and Mysticism* (New York: Oxford University Press, 1995), viii.

3. Grace Jantzen, *Julian of Norwich: Mystic and Theologian* (London: SPCK, 1987), 11.

4. Peter Dronke, preface to *Women Writers of the Middle Ages: A Critical Study of Texts from Perpetua to Marguerite Porete* (New York: Cambridge University Press, 1984), x.

5. Peter Brown, *The Body and Society: Men, Women, and Sexual Renunciation in Early Christianity* (London: Faber and Faber, 1989), 77.

6. Ibid., 80.

7. Pierre Abelard, *Historia Calamitatum,* trans. Betty Radice in *The Letters of Abelard and Heloise* (New York: Viking Penguin, Penguin Classics, 1974), 74.

8. Héloïse, letter to Abelard, trans. Betty Radice in *The Letters of Abelard and Heloise* (New York: Viking Penguin, Penguin Classics, 1974), 130–31.

9. Petroff, *Body and Soul,* 7.

10. Caroline W. Bynum, *Holy Feast and Holy Fast: The Religious Significance of Food to Medieval Women* (Berkeley, Calif.: University of California Press, 1987), 209–10.

11. Ibid.

12. Petroff, *Body and Soul,* 7.

13. Ibid., 205.

14. Dronke, *Women Writers,* 219–20.

15. Isaac Watts, *My Cheerful Soul* (London: Edward Arnold, 1962).

16. Marguerite Porete, trans. Peter Dronke in *Women Writers of the Middle Age: A Critical Study of Texts from Perpetua to Marguerite Porete* (New York: Cambridge University Press, 1984), 74.

# HÉLOÏSE

*ca.1100—ca.1163*

LITTLE IS KNOWN of Héloïse's early life except that her mother was called Hersinde and that it is possible Héloïse was illegitimate. She attended school at the convent of Argenteuil and must have had excellent teachers among the nuns, since she could write and read Greek, Latin, and Hebrew. When she finished school she lived with her uncle Fulbert, a canon of Notre Dame, as his ward.

Fulbert was proud of her intelligence and learning, and when she was seventeen he invited the great scholar Pierre Abelard to become her tutor. Abelard possessed an extraordinary intellectual caliber and a personal confidence that bordered on arrogance, which had already gained him a reputation as a firebrand. The eldest son of minor Breton nobility, he had renounced the life of a soldier to study philosophy, in particular dialectic, or logic. Attending the Cloister School of Notre Dame as a student, he out-argued his master, William of Champeaux, and set up his own school, which took pupils away from William. Later he went to Anselm of Laon to study theology, but quickly despising the method of proving theological points as if they were points of law, by quoting the saints and the Bible rather than trying to think ideas through, he fell out as bitterly with Anselm as he had with William. His fearless debating style, good looks, and brilliant intelligence brought him a passionate following among the young but made him a number of enemies in the ecclesiastical establishment, the most serious of whom was Bernard of Clairvaux, who felt Abelard's questioning style would undermine the basis of the Christian faith.

In a letter Abelard wrote to a friend much later in his life—the *Historia Calamitatum*—Abelard suggests that, having led a life of chastity until his thirties, he then made a cold decision to find a woman to seduce, and that his eye fell on Héloïse. Their relationship as teacher and pupil gave them unusual opportunities for closeness without chaperonage. Almost immediately they became lovers, and Abelard says that their "desires left no stage of love-making untried, and if love could devise something new, we welcomed it. We entered on each joy the more eagerly for our previous inexperience, and were the less easily sated."

Abelard began to neglect his work in the Schools, and songs he had written about Héloïse began to be sung all over Paris; gradually the scandal of his love affair with Héloïse became known. Belatedly Fulbert discovered what was going on. By this time Héloïse was pregnant, and Abelard took her, disguised as a nun, on a journey to live with his family in Brittany, where she would remain until the baby, Pierre Astrolabe, was born. Back in Paris, he went to Fulbert and offered to marry Héloïse on condition it could be kept secret. (Although Abelard was not in orders and so was technically free to marry—and in any case not all clergy were celibate at this period—marriage would have been thought damaging to his reputation as a philosopher.)

It was at this point that the strength of Héloïse's intelligence and character became clear. Her response to the idea of a marriage, secret or otherwise, was refusal. Neither she nor Abelard thought highly of marriage—it was widely regarded at the time as a regrettable compromise with the flesh—and her conviction was that they should remain together and give one another love just as long as they both wished to do so, that it should remain a union of total freedom. She feared that the cares of marriage and a family would destroy Abelard's energies and reputation as a philosopher. She also feared, rightly as it turned out, that Fulbert, who had shown himself full of sexual jealousy, was not to be trusted to keep the secret. She insisted that it filled her with pride to be Abelard's whore, as she put it—she asked no more of life. Although their way of life did not embrace the current form of romance—that of courtly love—the love of Héloïse has within it some of the same capacity to live out an extreme, and perhaps to invite self-destruction by doing so.

Persuaded by Abelard, Héloïse finally submitted to a secret marriage and afterward went to live at the convent of Argenteuil—her old school—where, at Abelard's suggestion, she wore the robe of a postulant. These devices were in vain. Possibly because he thought Abelard had discarded Héloïse and was now forcing her to become a nun, Fulbert arranged for men to force an entry into the master's rooms and castrate him.

In the uproar that followed this appalling event, Abelard arranged for Héloïse to return to the convent at Argenteuil and, after a relatively short lapse of time, to "take the veil." Perhaps she was too stunned by the scandal and tragedy that had overwhelmed her and Abelard to fully grasp what she was doing, perhaps she merely felt that this was some temporary device and that they would later be together again. As the years went by, she gradually realized the extent of her dereliction. She was appointed prioress of Argenteuil, the second in command at the convent, responsible for the education of pupils and much else.

After Héloïse had made her vows, Abelard himself became a monk at the Abbey of Saint Denis. His troubles, severe enough already, became worse. He was appalled by the laxity of life there and made himself unpopular by protesting. When he began to teach again, his enemies plotted against him, and his book about the Trinity was condemned and burned at the Council of Soissons. Abelard withdrew to a secluded rural area near Troyes, where he built a hermitage of reed and thatch, first dedicated to the Trinity but later to the Paraclete, the Comforter. There he was pursued by hundreds of students until he was obliged again to withdraw, and he became abbot of a monastery at Saint Gildas on a remote seacoast of Brittany.

In the meantime the Abbey of Saint Denis had evicted the nuns of Argenteuil, having found a claim to their land, and the sisters were homeless and destitute. Hearing of this, Abelard offered a group of them the use of the Paraclete, with Héloïse in charge as abbess; he traveled to Troyes to hand the property over to them. It was ten years since the couple had parted.

In a letter to Abelard from this period (the first letter,

which follows) Héloïse describes reading Abelard's account *Historia Calamitatum*, which somebody, not Abelard, had sent to her, and she complains bitterly of the way Abelard has abandoned her and the longing for him that still assails her. She accuses him roundly of having used her to fulfill his lust, and there is a coldness in the way he writes about her in the *Historia* that supports this view. As he recovered from the physical and mental trauma of his castration, Abelard had undergone a conversion process that led him to feel that his mutilation was deserved. Héloïse senses that he has moved away from her, but she has remained in the same place, loving and wanting Abelard just as she did before. Only her circumstances have changed, forcing on her the life of the convent but leaving her central passion untouched.

Of the two of her letters printed here, the first one contains an angry upbraiding of Abelard in which the pain of ten long, uncomprehending years spills out. It brought a reply from him not denying his love for her but making it clear that he could now only tolerate a rather distant brotherly relationship. In later letters Héloïse slowly began to recognize how total was the change in Abelard.

As she gradually accepts this she seems to move out of a state of helpless grieving, but it is important to her still to maintain contact with Abelard, and she defers to him in a number of ways, particularly in trying to work out how, as abbess at the Paraclete, she should adapt the Benedictine Rule intended for men for the use of her sisters. Some sort of regular contact with Abelard was established, with him occasionally visiting and writing to her. Her new role of abbess gave scope for her intellectual and other gifts.

She invited Abelard to write hymns and commentaries for the community.

Not only did he write hymns for them that later became famous, but he also offered detailed suggestions about the Rule as she had asked. The later Rule that was adopted by the nuns was in some ways stricter than Abelard suggested, but it is interesting that it did not accept his idea of the nuns being ruled by a male superior (as part of a double monastery of men and women) but rather placed the abbess in charge of her sisters. The influence here is plainly Héloïse's. In her rejection both of total enclosure and of male jurisdiction she prefigures Clare's reforms.

Perhaps partly because of guilt over "the calamity," Héloïse feels a need to deplore being a woman. She lectures Abelard about the women in history who have brought about the downfall of great men (ironically, since she need look no further than her own life to see that women were equally ruined by unlucky association). Abelard makes no attempt to counter her deprecation of women in his letters—it must have seemed an entirely natural way to speak. He himself repeatedly mentions the "weakness" of women (he means psychological and spiritual weakness as well as the physical kind).

All the same, as befitted a well-known abbess, Héloïse actually writes with great confidence, shrewdness, sometimes with truculence—there is nothing timid about her—and judging by her written style she must have been a formidable woman, partly because of her fine intelligence and perhaps partly because of the baptism of fire in her youth. Abelard selected a woman who could hold her own with him.

Her spirituality is not of the mystical kind. She is frank about the fact that when she entered the convent she did it not for the love of God, whom she believed she had deeply offended, but for the love of Abelard. In that spirit she had taken her vows. Yet in caring for the sisters, designing the framework of manual work and prayer that made up their life, supervising the school, caring for the poor and sick who came to the sisters for help, she seems to have found a way for herself, a way of distinction and grace. She was clearly admired by contemporary men of spiritual gifts, such as Peter the Venerable.

## FIRST LETTER FROM HÉLOÏSE TO ABELARD

*This letter contains the outpourings of ten years in which Héloïse has not seen or spoken to Abelard, and until she reads his* Historia Calamitatum, *she has no idea of how he has lived with the catastrophe that engulfed them both. Reading it, she is appalled at the coldness toward her that she finds there; it contrasts unbearably with the love and longing she has felt for him in the years in the convent. She has an acute sense of the unfairness of his attitude, since everything she has done, including entering the convent, she has done out of loyalty to him.*

To her master, or rather her father, husband, or rather brother; his handmaid, or rather his daughter, wife, or rather sister; to Abelard, Héloïse.

Not long ago, my beloved, by chance someone brought me the letter of consolation you had sent to a friend. I saw at once from the superscription that it was yours, and was all the more eager to read it since the writer is so dear to my heart. I hoped for renewal of strength, at least from the writer's words, which would picture for me the reality I have lost. But nearly every line of this letter was filled, I remember, with gall and wormwood, as it told the pitiful story of our entry into religion and the cross of unending suffering which you, my only love, continue to bear.

In that letter you did indeed carry out the promise you made your friend at the beginning, that he would think his own troubles insignificant or nothing in comparison with your own. First you revealed the persecution you suffered from your teachers, then the supreme treachery of the mutilation of your person, and then described the abominable jealousy and violent attacks of your fellow students, Alberic of Rheims and Lotulf of Lombardy. You did not gloss over what at their instigation was done to your distinguished theological work or what amounted to a prison sentence passed on yourself. Then you went on to the plotting against you by your abbot and false brethren, the serious slanders from those two pseudoapostles, spread against you by the same rivals, and the scandal stirred up among many people because you had acted contrary to custom in naming your oratory after the Paraclete. You went on to the incessant, intolerable persecutions which you still endure at the hands of that cruel tyrant and the evil monks you call your sons, and so brought your sad story to an end.

No one, I think, could read or hear it dry-eyed; my own sorrows are renewed by the detail in which you have told it, and redoubled because you say your perils are still increasing. All of us here are driven to despair of your life, and every day we await in fear and trembling the final word of your death. And so in the name of Christ, who is still giving you some protection for his service, we beseech you to write as often as you think fit to us who are his handmaids and yours, with news of the perils in which you are still storm-tossed. We are all that are left you, so at least you should let us share your sorrow or your joy.

It is always some consolation in sorrow to feel that it is shared, and any burden laid on several is carried more lightly or removed. And if this storm has quietened down for a while, you must be all the more prompt to send us a letter which will be the more gladly received. . . .

You wrote your friend a long letter of consolation, prompted no doubt by his misfortunes, but really telling of your own. The detailed account you gave of these may have been intended for his comfort, but it also greatly increased our own feeling of desolation; in your desire to heal his wounds you have dealt us fresh wounds of grief as well as reopening the old. I beg you, then, as you set about tending the wounds which others have dealt, heal the wounds you have yourself inflicted. You have done your duty to a friend and comrade, discharged your debt to friendship and comradeship, but it is a greater debt which binds you in obligation to us who can properly be called not friends so much as dearest friends, not comrades but daughters, or any other conceivable name more tender and holy. How great the debt by which you have bound yourself to us needs neither proof nor witness, were it in any doubt; if the whole world kept silent, the facts themselves would cry out. For you after God are the sole founder of this place, the sole builder of this oratory, the sole creator of this community. You have built nothing here upon another man's foundation. Everything here is your own creation. This was a wilderness open to wild beasts and brigands, a place which had known no home nor habitation of men. In the very lairs of wild beasts and lurking-places of robbers, where the name of God was never heard, you built a sanctuary to God and dedicated a shrine in the name of the Holy Spirit. To build it you drew nothing from the riches of kings and princes, though their wealth was great and could have been yours for the asking: whatever was done, the credit was to be yours alone. Clerks and scholars came flocking here, eager for your teaching, and ministered to all your needs; and even those who had lived on the benefices of the Church and knew only how to receive offerings, not to make them, whose hands were held out to take but not to give, became pressing in their lavish offers of assistance.

As so it is yours, truly your own, this new plantation for God's purpose, but it is sown with plants which are still very tender and need watering if they are to thrive. Through its feminine nature this plantation would be weak and frail even if it were not new; and so it needs a more careful and regular cultivation, according to the words of the Apostle: "I planted the seed and Apollos watered it; but God made it grow." The Apostle, through the doctrine that he preached, had planted and established in the faith the Corinthians, to whom he was writing. Afterward the Apostle's own disciple, Apollos, had watered them with his holy exhortations and so God's grace bestowed on them growth in the virtues. You cultivate a vineyard of another's vines, which you did not plant yourself and which has now turned to bitterness against you, so that often your advice brings no result and your holy words are uttered in vain. You devote your care to another's vineyard; think what you owe to your own. You teach and admonish rebels to no purpose, and in vain you throw the pearls of your divine eloquence to the pigs. While you spend so much on the stubborn, consider what you owe to the obedient; you are so generous to your enemies but should reflect on how you are indebted to your daughters. Apart from everything else, consider the close tie by which you have bound yourself to me, and repay the debt you owe a whole community of women dedicated to God by discharging it the more dutifully to her who is yours alone.

Your superior wisdom knows better than our humble learning of the many serious treatises which the holy Fathers compiled for the instruction or exhortation or even the consolation of holy women, and of the care with which these were composed. And so in the precarious early days of our conversion long ago I was not a little surprised and troubled by your forgetfulness, when neither reverence for God nor our mutual love nor the example of the holy Fathers made you think of trying to comfort me, wavering and exhausted as I was by prolonged grief, either by word when I was with you or by letter when we had parted. Yet you must know that you are bound to me by an obligation which is all the greater for the further close tie of the marriage sacrament uniting us, and are the deeper in my debt because of the love I have always borne you, as everyone knows, a love which is beyond all bounds.

You know, beloved, as the whole world knows, how much I have lost in you, how at one wretched stroke of fortune that supreme act of flagrant treachery robbed me of my very self in robbing me of you, and how my sorrow for my loss is nothing compared with what I feel for the manner in which I lost you. Surely the greater the cause for grief the greater the need for the help of consolation, and this no one can bring but you; you are the sole cause of my sorrow, and you alone can grant me the grace of consolation. You alone have the power to make me sad, to being me happiness or comfort; you alone have so great a debt to repay me, particularly now when I have carried out all your orders so implicitly that when I was powerless to oppose you in anything, I found strength at your command to destroy myself. I did more, strange to say—my love rose to such heights of madness that it robbed itself of what it most desired beyond hope of recovery, when immediately at your bidding I changed my clothing along with my mind, in order to prove you the sole possessor of my body and my will alike. God knows I never sought anything in you except yourself; I wanted simply you, nothing of yours. I looked for no marriage bond, no marriage portion, and it was not my own pleasures and wishes I sought to gratify, as you well know, but yours. The name of wife may seem more sacred or more binding, but sweeter for me will always be the word mistress, or, if you will permit me, that of concubine or whore. I believed that the more I humbled myself on your account, the more gratitude I should win from you, and also the less damage I should do the brightness of your reputation.

You yourself on your own account did not altogether forget this in the letter of consolation I have spoken of which you wrote to a friend; there you thought fit to set out some of the reasons I gave in trying to dissuade you from binding us together in an ill-starred marriage. But you kept silent about most of my arguments for preferring love to wedlock and freedom to chains. God is my witness that if Augustus, emperor of the whole world, thought fit to honor me with marriage and conferred all the earth on me to possess forever, it would be dearer and more honorable to me to be called not his empress but your whore.

For a man's worth does not rest on his wealth or power; these depend on fortune, but worth on his merits. And a woman should realize that if she marries a rich man more readily than a poor one, and desires her husband more for his possessions than for himself, she is offering herself for sale. Certainly any woman who comes to marry through desires of this kind deserves wages, not gratitude, for clearly her mind is on the man's property, not himself, and she would be ready to prostitute herself to a richer man, if she could. This is evident from the argument put forward in the dialogue of Aeschines Socraticus by the learned Aspasia to Xenophon and his wife. When she had expounded it in an effort to bring about a reconciliation between them, she ended with these words: "Unless you come to believe that there is no better man nor worthier woman on earth you will always still be looking for what you judge the best thing of all—to be the husband of the best of wives and the wife of the best of husbands."

These are saintly words which are more than philosophic; indeed, they deserve the name of wisdom, not philosophy. It is a holy error and a blessed delusion between man and wife, when perfect love can keep the ties of marriage unbroken not so much through bodily continence as chastity of spirit. But what error permitted other women, plain truth permitted me, and what they thought of their husbands, the world in general believed, or rather, knew, to be true of yourself; so that my love for you was the more genuine for being further removed from error. What king or philosopher could match your fame? What district,

town, or village did not long to see you? When you appeared in public, who did not hurry to catch a glimpse of
you, or crane his neck and strain his eyes to follow your
departure? Every wife, every young girl, desired you in absence and was on fire in your presence; queens and great
ladies envied me my joys and my bed.

You had besides, I admit, two special gifts whereby to
win at once the heart of any woman—your gifts for composing verse and song, in which we know other philoso-
phers have rarely been successful. This was for you no
more than a diversion, a recreation from the labors of your
philosophic work, but you left many love songs and verses
which won wide popularity for the charm of their words
and tunes and kept your name continually on everyone's
lips. The beauty of the airs ensured that even the unlettered
did not forget you; more than anything this made women
sigh for love of you. And as most of these songs told of
our love, they soon made me widely known and roused
the envy of many women against me. For your manhood
was adorned by every grace of mind and body, and among
the women who envied me then, could there be one now
who does not feel compelled by my misfortune to sympa-
thize with my loss of such joys? Who is there who was
once my enemy, whether man or woman, who is not
moved now by the compassion which is my due? Wholly
guilty though I am, I am also, as you know, wholly innocent. It is not the deed but the intention of the doer which
makes the crime, and justice should weigh not what was
done but the spirit in which it is done. What my intention
toward you has always been, you alone who have known
it can judge. I submit all to your scrutiny, yield to your
testimony in all things.

Tell me one thing, if you can. Why, after our entry into religion, which was your decision alone, have I been so neglected and forgotten by you that I have neither a word from you when you are here to give me strength nor the consolation of a letter in absence? Tell me, I say, if you can—or I will tell you what I think and indeed the world suspects. It was desire, not affection, which bound you to me, the flame of lust rather than love. So when the end came to what you desired, any show of feeling you used to make went with it. This is not merely my own opinion, beloved, it is everyone's. There is nothing personal or private about it; it is the general view which is widely held. I only wish that it *were* mine alone, and that the love you professed could find someone to defend it and so comfort me in my grief for a while. I wish I could think of some explanation which would excuse you and somehow cover up the way you hold me cheap.

I beg you then to listen to what I ask—you will see that is a small favor which you can easily grant. While I am denied your presence, give me at least through your words—of which you have enough and to spare—some sweet semblance of yourself. It is no use my hoping for generosity in deeds if you are grudging in words. Up to now I had thought I deserved much of you, seeing that I carried out everything for your sake and continue up to the present moment in complete obedience to you. It was not any sense of vocation which brought me as a young girl to accept the austerities of the cloister, but your bidding alone, and if I deserve no gratitude from you, you may judge for yourself how my labors are in vain. I can expect no reward for this from God, for it is certain that I have done nothing as yet for love of him. When you hurried toward God I followed you; indeed, I went first to take the veil—perhaps you were thinking how Lot's wife turned back, when you made me put on the religious habit and take my vows before you gave yourself to God. Your lack of trust in me over this one thing, I confess, overwhelmed me with grief and shame. I would have had no hesitation, God knows, in following you or going ahead at your bidding to the flames of Hell. My heart was not in me but with you, and now even more, if it is not with you it is nowhere; truly, without you it cannot exist. See that it fares well with you, I beg, as it will if it finds you kind, if you give grace in return for grace, small for great, words for deeds. If only your love had less confidence in me, my dear, so that you would be more concerned on my behalf! But as it is, the more I have made you feel secure in me, the more I have to bear with your neglect.

Remember, I implore you, what I have done, and think how much you owe me. While I enjoyed with you the pleasures of the flesh, many were uncertain whether I was prompted by love or lust; but now the end is proof of the beginning. I have finally denied myself every pleasure in obedience to your will, kept nothing for myself except to prove that now, even more, I am yours. Consider then your injustice, if when I deserve more you give me less, or rather, nothing at all, especially when it is a small thing I ask of you and one you could so easily grant. And so, in the name of God to whom you have dedicated yourself, I beg you to restore your presence to me in the way you can—by writing me some word of comfort, so that in this at least I may find increased strength and readiness to serve God. When in the past you sought me out for sinful pleasures, your letters came to me thick and fast, and your many songs put your Héloïse on everyone's lips, so that every street and house echoed with my name. Is it not far better now to summon me to God than it was then to satisfy our lust? I beg you, think what you owe me, give ear to my pleas, and I will finish a long letter with a brief ending: farewell, my only love.

## SECOND LETTER FROM HÉLOÏSE TO ABELARD

*In her second letter, replying to Abelard's response to her first, Héloïse is still full of unruly feelings— "unbounded grief," as she says. The renewal of contact between them has unloosed a flood of pain and recrimination. She is determined to keep the link between them open by one means or another, and her method is to seek Abelard's advice on many matters to do with the life of the Paraclete.*

I would not want to give you cause for finding me disobedient in anything, so I have set the bridle of your injunction on the words which issue from my unbounded grief; thus in writing at least I may moderate what it is difficult or rather impossible to forestall in speech. For nothing is less under our control than the heart—having no power to command it we are forced to obey. And so when its impulses move us, none of us can stop their sudden promptings from easily breaking out and even more easily overflowing into words which are the ever-ready indications of the heart's emotions: as it is written, "A man's words are spoken from the overflowing of the heart." I will therefore hold my hand from writing words which I cannot restrain my tongue from speaking; would that a grieving heart would be as ready to obey as a writer's hand! And yet you have it in your power to remedy my grief, even if you cannot entirely remove it. As one nail drives out another hammered in, a new thought expels an old when the mind is intent on other things and forced to dismiss or interrupt its recollection of the past. But the more fully any thought occupies the mind and distracts it from other things, the more worthy should be the subject of such a thought and the more important it is where we direct our minds.

And so all we handmaids of Christ, who are your daughters in Christ, come as suppliants to demand of your paternal interest two things which we see to be very necessary for ourselves. One is that you will teach us how the order of nuns began and what authority there is for our profession. The other, that you will prescribe some Rule for us and write it down, a Rule which shall be suitable for women, and also describe fully the manner and habit of our way of life, which we find was never done by the holy Fathers. Through lack and need of this it is the practice today for men and women alike to be received into monasteries to profess the same Rule, and the same yoke of monastic ordinance is laid on the weaker sex as on the stronger.

At present the one Rule of Saint Benedict is professed in the Latin Church by women equally with men, although, as it was clearly written for men alone, it can only be fully obeyed by men, whether subordinates or superiors. Leaving aside for the moment the other articles of the Rule: How can women be concerned with what is written there about cowls, drawers, or scapulars? Or indeed, with tunics or woolen garments worn next to the skin, when the monthly purging of their superfluous humors must avoid such things? How are they affected by the ruling of the abbot, that he shall read aloud the Gospel himself and afterward start the hymn? What about the abbot's table, set apart for him with pilgrims and guests? Which is more fitting for our religious life: for an abbess never to offer hospitality to men, or for her to eat with men she has allowed in? It is all too easy for the souls of men and women to be destroyed if they live together in one place, and especially at table, where gluttony and drunkenness are rife, and wine which leads to lechery is drunk with enjoyment. . . .

To pass over these provisions of the Rule which we are unable to observe in detail, or cannot observe without danger to ourselves: What about gathering in the harvest—has it ever been the custom for convents of nuns to go out to do this, or to tackle the work of the fields? Again, are we to test the constancy of the women we receive during the space of a single year and instruct them by three readings of the Rule, as it says there? What could be so foolish as to set out on an unknown path, not yet defined, or so presumptuous as to choose and profess a way of life of which you know nothing, or to take a vow you are not capable of keeping? And since discretion is the mother of all the virtues and reason the mediator of all that is good, who will judge anything virtuous or good which is seen to conflict with discretion and reason? For the virtues which exceed all bounds and measure are, as Jerome says, to be counted among vices. It is clearly contrary to reason and discretion if burdens are imposed without previous investigation into the strength of those who are to bear them, to ensure that human industry may depend on natural constitution. . . .

Certainly those who laid down rules for monks were not only completely silent about women but also prescribed regulations which they knew to be quite unsuitable for them. . . .

Consider then how far removed it is from all reason and good sense if both women and men are bound by profession of a common Rule, and the same burden is laid on the weak as on the strong. I think it should be sufficient for our infirmity if the virtue of continence and also of abstinence makes us the equals of the rulers of the Church themselves and of the clergy who are confirmed in holy orders. . . .

As regards fasts, which Christians hold to be abstinence from vices rather than from food, you must consider whether anything should be added to what the Church has instituted, and order what is suitable for us.

But it is chiefly in connection with the offices of the Church and ordering of the psalms that provision is needed, so that here at least, if you think fit, you may allow some concession to our weakness, and when we recite the psalter in full within a week it shall not be necessary to repeat the same psalms. When Saint Benedict divided up the week according to his view, he left instructions that others could order the psalms differently, if it seemed better to do so, for he expected that with passage of time the ceremonies of the Church would become more elaborate, and from a rough foundation would arise a splended edifice.

Above all, we want you to decide what we ought to do about reading the Gospel in the Night Office. It seems to us hazardous if priests and deacons, who should perform the reading, are allowed among us at such hours, when we should be especially segregated from the approach and sight of men in order to devote ourselves more sincerely to God and to be safer from temptation.

It is for you then, master, while you live, to lay down for us what Rule we are to follow for all time, for after God you are the founder of this place, through God you are the creator of our community, with God you should be the director of our religious life. After you we may perhaps have another to guide us, one who will build something upon another's foundation, and so, we fear, he may be less likely to feel concern for us, or be less readily heard by us; or indeed, he may be no less willing but less able. Speak to us then, and we shall hear. Farewell.

**CHRISTINA**
**of MARKYATE**
*ca.1096–ca.1166*

THEODORA WAS the eldest child of a rich and noble couple in Huntingdon, Autti and Beatrix. During her pregnancy Beatrix became convinced that she was going to give birth to a special child. As she looked out the window one day toward the monastery of Our Lady, "she saw a dove, whiter than snow, leave the monastery and come straight towards her in a gentle flight; and with its wings folded, it took shelter in the sleeve of the tunic she was wearing. . . . The dove stayed quietly with her for seven whole days, allowing itself to be stroked with her hands, showing no sign of uneasiness, and nestling comfortably and with evident pleasure first in her lap and then in her bosom." This remarkable event suggested to both Beatrix and Christina's biographer that the coming child would be filled with the Holy Spirit. It is reminiscent of the experience of the mother of Hilda of Whitby, who, in pregnancy, had a dream that she had a jewel beneath her gown that shone with a brilliant light. Both mothers had great hopes for their unborn children, which perhaps itself later encouraged the children to be remarkable. For girls, for whom there were such limited expectations, this may have been particularly significant.

Unfortunately, Theodora's mother did not like the form that her daughter's spiritual development took. As a young girl Theodora made a vow of virginity, when she visited Saint Albans and was attracted by monastic life there. This led her to refuse an early marriage to an eligible nobleman, Burthred. Beatrix and Autti shut Christina up, bullied and abused her, sometimes in public, and bribed other girls to try to persuade her into marriage. Finally, worn out by the pressure, Christina agreed to "espousal" with Burthred; fearful she might change her mind, they smuggled him into her bedroom to consummate the union before she could have second thoughts.

In the end, helped by the intervention of a hermit, Eadwin, Christina, as she was now known (it was the name she adopted for her new life), ran away and remained hidden in the cell of Alfwen of Flamstead for many months. Later Burthred absolved her from the marriage, and the church annulled the union. After the death of Robert Bloet, the bishop of Lincoln, who was an enemy of Christina's, she lived as a recluse at Markyate, making a monastic profession at Saint Albans. Geoffrey, the abbot, became a friend to her.

## THE LIFE OF SAINT THEODORA, WHO IS ALSO CALLED CHRISTINA

*An unknown monk, possibly Abbot Thomas De La Mare, wrote down Christina's story in a style that*

*suggested he was captivated by the drama and cour-*
*age of it.*

In the town of Huntingdon there was born into a family
of noble rank a maiden of uncommon holiness and beauty.
Her father's name was Autti, her mother's Beatrix. The
name which she herself had been given in baptism was
Theodora, but later on, through force of circumstance, she
changed it to Christina. . . .

The child grew and was weaned, and as it grew in
strength so it made progress in virtue. Hence it came about
that while she was still too young to see the difference between right and wrong, she beat her own tender body with
rods whenever she thought she had done something that
was not allowed. But even so the child was still unable to
understand why she should love righteousness and hate
wickedness. In the meantime, as she had heard that Christ
was good, beautiful, and everywhere present, she used to
talk to Him on her bed at night just as if she were speaking
to a man she could see; and this she did with a loud clear
voice, so that all who were resting in the same house could
hear and understand her. She thought that if she were
speaking to God, she could not be heard by man. But
when they made fun of her, she changed this mode of acting. . . .

In the meantime, by an act of divine providence, Autti
and Beatrix brought their dear daughter Christina with
them to our monastery of the blessed martyr Saint Alban,
where his sacred bones are revered, to beg his protection
for themselves and for their child. When the girl therefore
had looked carefully at the place and observed the religious bearing of the monks who dwelt there, she declared

how fortunate the inmates were, and expressed a wish to share in their fellowship. At length, as her parents were leaving the monastery, having fulfilled all the things they had come to do, she made a sign of the cross with one of her fingernails on the door as a token that she had placed her affection there. . . . The following day she went to the church where the priest was saying Mass. After the Gospel Christina approached the altar and offered a penny, saying in her heart, "O Lord God, merciful and all powerful, receive my oblation through the hands of Thy priest. For to Thee as a surrender of myself I offer this penny. Grant me, I beseech Thee, purity and inviolable virginity whereby Thou mayest renew in me the image of Thy Son, who lives and reigns with Thee in the unity of the Holy Spirit God for ever and ever, amen." . . .

Christina remained peacefully in her father's house, rejoicing that she could grow from day to day in holy virtue and in the love of supernatural things. But the envy of the devil could not long endure this, and burning with desire to upset her, took the initiative in this way. While Ralph the bishop of Durham was justiciar of the whole of England, holding the second place after the king, but before he became a bishop, he had taken to himself Christina's maternal aunt, named Alveva, and had children by her. Afterward he gave her in marriage to one of the citizens of Huntingdon and for her sake held the rest of her kin in high esteem. On his way from Northumbria to London and on his return from there he always lodged with her. On one occasion when he was there, Autti, his friend, had come as usual with his children to see him. The bishop gazed intently at his beautiful daughter, and immediately Satan put it into his heart to desire her. Busily, therefore, seeking some trick of getting her into his power, he had the unsuspecting girl brought into his chamber where he himself slept, which was hung with beautiful tapestries, the only others present with the innocent child being members of his retinue. Her father and mother and the others with whom she had come were in the hall apart, giving themselves up to drunkenness. When it was getting dark the bishop gave a secret sign to his servants and they left the room, leaving their master and Christina, that is to say, the wolf and the lamb, together in the same room. For shame! The shameless bishop took hold of Christina by one of the sleeves of her tunic and with that mouth which he used to consecrate the sacred species, he solicited her to commit a wicked deed. What was the poor girl to do in such straits? Should she call her parents? They had already gone to bed. To consent was out of the question, but openly resist she dared not because if she openly resisted him, she would certainly be overcome by force.

Hear, then, how prudently she acted. She glanced toward the door and saw that, though it was closed, it was not bolted. And she said to him, "Allow me to bolt the door: for even if we have no fear of God, at least we should take precautions that no man should catch us in this act." He demanded an oath from her that she would not deceive him, but that she would, as she said, bolt the door. And she swore to him. And so, being released, she darted out of the room and, bolting the door firmly from the outside, hurried quickly home. This was the beginning of all the frightful troubles that followed afterward. Then that wretch, seeing that he had been made a fool of by a young girl, was eaten up with resentment and counted all his power as nothing until he could avenge the insult he had suffered. But the only way in which he could conceivably gain his revenge was by depriving Christina of her virginity, either by himself or by someone else, for the preservation of which she did not hesitate to repulse even a bishop.

. . . He spoke to a young nobleman named Burthred, egging him on to ask for Christina's hand in marriage, promising that he would further his request by every means in his power. When the young man acted on the bishop's advice, the bishop backed his promise with such malicious persistence that he did not stop until, against Christina's will, he had gained the parents' consent for her to be betrothed to Burthred. When this was accomplished, the prelate, glorying in his conquest, went off to Durham, leaving the maiden sad at heart in her parents' home. After this the aforesaid young man called on her father and mother to arrange his betrothal with the girl who they had promised should be his wife. When they spoke to her about preparations for the wedding, she would not listen. And when they asked the reason, she replied, "I wish to remain single, for I have made a vow of virginity." On hearing this, they made fun of her rashness. But she remained unmoved by it; therefore they tried to convince her of her foolishness and, despite her rejections, encouraged her to hurry on the marriage preparations. She refused. They brought her gifts and made great promises; she brushed them aside. They cajoled her; they threatened her; but she would not yield. . . . Sometime later, however, when they were all gathered together in the church, they made a concerted and sudden attack on her. To be brief, how it happened I cannot tell. All I know is that by God's will, with so many exerting pressure on her from all sides, she yielded (at least in word), and on that very day Bur-thred was betrothed to her.

After the espousal the maiden returned once more to her parents' home while her husband, though he had houses elsewhere, built her a new and larger dwelling-place near his father-in-law. But although she was married, her former intentions were not changed, and she freely ex-pressed her determination not to submit to the physical embraces of any man. The more her parents became aware of her persistence in this frame of mind, the more they tried to break down her resistance, first by flattery, then by reproaches, sometimes by presents and grand promises, and even by threats and punishment. And though all her friends and relatives united forces together in this purpose, her father Autti surpassed them all in his efforts, while he himself was outclassed by the girl's mother, as will become evident later on. After they had tried out many methods without result, they finally hit on this subterfuge. Putting her under strict and rigorous guard, they prevented any religious, god-fearing man from having any conversation with her; on the other hand, they freely invited to the house people given to jesting, boasting, worldly amuse-ment, and those whose evil communications corrupt good manners. Furthermore, they stopped her going to the mon-astery of Our Lady because it became apparent that when-ever she paid a visit there she came back confirmed and strengthened in her resolution. This was very hard for her to bear, and to those who forbade her she said with great feeling, "Even though you may deny me access to the mon-astery of my beloved Lady, you cannot wrench its memory from my breast." They forbade her access to the chapel which was most dear to her and would not allow her to go to that place. But they took her with them, against her will, to public banquets, where divers choice meats were followed by drinks of different kinds, where the alluring melodies of the singers were accompanied by the sounds of the zither and the harp, so that by listening to them her strength of mind might be sapped away and in this way she might finally be brought to take pleasure in the world. But their wiles were outwitted at all points and served but to emphasize her invincible prudence. . . .

As her parents had been outwitted in this, they tried something else. And at night they let her husband secretly into her bedroom in order that, if he found the maiden asleep, he might suddenly take her by surprise and overcome her. But even through that providence to which she had commended herself, she was found dressed and awake, and she welcomed the young man as if he had been her brother. And sitting on her bed with him, she strongly encouraged him to live a chaste life, putting forward the saints as examples. . . . "Do not take it amiss that I have declined your embraces. In order that your friends may not reproach you with being rejected by me, I will go home with you, and let us live together there for some time, ostensibly as husband and wife, but in reality living chastely in the sight of the Lord. But first let us join hands in a compact that neither meanwhile will touch the other unchastely, neither will look upon the other except with a pure and angelic gaze, making a promise that in three or four years' time we will receive the religious habit and offer ourselves . . . to some monastery which providence shall appoint." When the greater part of the night had passed with talk such as this, the young man eventually left the maiden. When those who had got him into the room heard what had happened, they joined together in calling him a spineless and useless fellow. And with many reproaches they goaded him on again, and thrust him into her bedroom another night, having warned him not to be misled by her deceitful tricks and naive words nor to lose his manliness. Either by force or entreaty he was to gain his end. And if neither of these sufficed, he was to know that they were at hand to help him: all he had to mind was to act the man.

When Christina sensed this, she hastily sprang out of bed and clinging with both hands to a nail which was fixed in the wall, she hung trembling between the wall and the hangings. Burthred meanwhile approached the bed and, not finding what he expected, he immediately gave a sign to those waiting outside the door. They crowded into the room forthwith and with lights in their hands ran from place to place looking for her, the more intent on their quest as they knew she was in the room when he entered it and could not have escaped without their seeing her. What, I ask you, were her feelings at that moment? How she kept trembling as they noisily sought after her. Was she not faint with fear? She saw herself already dragged out in their midst, all surrounding her, looking upon her, threatening her, given up to the sport of her destroyer. At last one of them touched and held her foot as she hung there, but since the curtain in between deadened his sense of touch, he let it go, not knowing what it was. Then the maiden of Christ, taking courage, prayed to God, saying, "Let them be turned backward, that desire my hurt," and straightway they departed in confusion, and from that moment she was safe.

Nevertheless, Burthred entered her room a third time

in a similar state of agitated fury. But as he came in one door, she fled through another. In front of her was a kind of fence which, because of its height and the sharp spikes on top of it, was calculated to prevent anyone from climbing over it; behind her almost on her heels was the young man, who at any moment would catch hold of her. With amazing ease she jumped over the fence and, looking back from her place of safety, saw her pursuer on the other side, standing there unable to follow. Then she said, "Truly in escaping him, I have escaped from the devil I saw last night." For, in her sleep, she had seen as it were a devil of horrible appearance with blackened teeth who was unavailingly trying to seize her, because in her flight she had sprung at one leap over a high fence. While her parents were setting these and other traps for her, they fixed the day for the marriage with their son-in-law several times. For they hoped that some occasion would arise when they could take advantage of her. For what woman could hope to escape so many snares? And yet, with Christ guarding the vow which his spouse had made, the celebration of the wedding could nohow be brought about. Indeed, when the day which they had fixed approached and all the necessary preparations for the marriage had been arranged, it happened first that all the things prepared were burned by an unexpected fire, and then that the bride was taken with fever. In order to drive away the fever, sometimes they thrust her into cold water, at other times they blistered her excessively. . . .

Her father placed her before Fredebert, the reverend prior, and the rest of the canons of the house, and addressed them with these doleful words: "I know, my fathers, I know, and I admit to my daughter, that I and her

mother have forced her against her will into this marriage
and that against her better judgment she has received this
sacrament. Yet, no matter how she was led into it, if she
resists our authority and rejects it, we shall be the laugh-
ingstock of our neighbors, a mockery and derision to those
who are round about. Wherefore, I beseech you, plead
with her to have pity on us: let her marry in the Lord and
take away our reproach. Why must she depart from tradition? Why should she bring this dishonor on her father?
Her life of poverty will bring the whole of the nobility into
disrepute. Let her do now what we wish, and she can have
all that we possess." When Autti had said this, Fredebertus
asked him to leave the assembly and with his canons about
him began to address the maiden with these words: "We
are surprised, Theodora, at your obstinacy, or rather we
should say, your madness. We know that you have been
betrothed according to ecclesiastical custom. We know
that the sacrament of marriage, which has been sanctioned
by divine law, cannot be dissolved, because what God has
joined together, no man should put asunder. For this a
man will leave his father and mother and cleave to his
wife. And they shall be two in one flesh. And the Apostle
says: Let the husband render unto the wife due benevo-
lence and likewise also the wife unto the husband. The
woman has no power over her own body, but the husband; and likewise also the husband has not power over
his own body, but the wife. Unto the married I command,
yet not I, but the Lord, let not the wife depart from her
husband and let not the husband put away his wife. And
we know the commandment given to children: Obey your
parents and show them respect. These two command-
ments, about obedience to parents and faithfulness in mar-

riage, are great, much commended in the Old and New Testaments. Yet the bond of marriage is so much more important than the authority of parents that if they commanded you to break off the marriage, you should not listen to them. Now, however, that they order you to do something which we know on divine authority to be more important than obedience itself, and you do not listen to them, you are doubly at fault. Nor should you think that only virgins are saved: for while many virgins perish, many mothers of families are saved, as we well know. And since this is so, nothing remains but that you accept our advice and teaching and submit yourself to the lawful embraces of the man to whom you have been legally joined in marriage."

To these exhortations Christina replied: "I am ignorant of the scriptures which you have quoted, father prior. But from their sense I will give my answers thereto. My father and mother, as you have heard, bear me witness that against my will this sacrament, as you call it, was forced on me. I have never been a wife and have never thought of becoming one. Know that from my infancy I have chosen chastity and have vowed to Christ that I would remain a virgin; this I did before witnesses, but even if they were not present, God would be witness to my conscience continuously. This I showed by my actions as far as I was allowed. And if my parents have ordered me to enter into a marriage which I never wanted and to break the vow to Christ which they know I made in my childhood, I leave you, who are supposed to excel other men in the knowledge of the scriptures, to judge how wicked a thing this is. If I do all in my power to fulfill the vow I made to Christ, I shall not be disobedient to my parents. What I do, I do on the invitation of Him whose voice, as you say, is heard in the Gospel: Every one who leaves house or brothers or sisters or father or mother or wife or children or possessions for My name's sake shall receive a hundredfold and possess eternal life. Nor do I think that virgins only will be saved. But I say as you do, and it is true, that if many virgins perish, so rather do married women. And if many mothers of families are saved, which you likewise say, and it is true, certainly virgins are saved more easily."

Fredebertus, astonished at the common sense and answers of Christina, asked her, saying: "How do you prove to me that you are doing this for the love of Christ? Perhaps you are rejecting marriage with Burthred in order to enter a more wealthy one?" "A more wealthy one, certainly," she replied. "For who is richer than Christ?" Then said he, "I am not joking. I am treating with you seriously. And if you wish us to believe you, take an oath in our presence that, were you betrothed to him as you have been to Burthred, you would not marry even the king's son." At these words the maiden, casting her eyes up to heaven and with a joyful countenance, replied, "I will not merely take an oath, but I am prepared to prove it, by carrying red-hot iron in these my bare hands. For, as I have frequently declared, I must fulfill the vow which through the inspiration of His grace I made to the only Son of the Eternal King, and with the help of this same grace I mean to fulfill it. And I trust to God that the time is not far off when it will become clear that I have no other in view but Christ."

Fredebertus then called in Autti and said to him, "We have tried our best to bend your daughter to your will, but we have made no headway. We know, however, that our

bishop, Robert, will be coming soon to his village at Buckden, which is near this town. Reason demands that the
whole question should be laid before him. Let the case be
put into his hands after he comes and let her take the verdict of the bishop, if of no other. What is the point of tear-
ing your vitals and suffering to no purpose? We respect the
high resolution of this maiden as founded on impregnable
virtue." To which Autti replied, "I accept your advice.
Please seek the bishop on this affair." He agreed, and so
Autti brought back his daughter and placed her under the
usual restraint.

In the meantime he heard that the bishop had come to
Buckden. Fredebertus immediately sought him out, being
sent by Autti, and with him went the most noble citizens
of the town, who thought that, as the marriage had already been performed, the bishop would immediately
order the betrothed woman to submit to the authority of
her husband. Hence they laid before him in detail and
without delay all the facts which they knew pertained to
the business in hand, namely what Christina had done,
what others had done to her, beginning with her childhood
and bringing it up to the present day. At last they brought
forward the proposal . . . that since neither adversity nor
prosperity could bring her to it she should be forced to
accept her marriage at least by episcopal authority. After
weighing all the evidence minutely, the bishop said, "I de-
clare to you, and I swear before God and His blessed
Mother that there is no bishop under heaven who could
force her into marriage, if according to her vow she wishes
to keep herself for God to serve Him freely and for no man
besides." Hearing this unexpected answer, they returned
in confusion and reported the bishop's reply to Autti.

When he heard it, he lost all hope; and full of self-pity, but more to be pitied, he said to Christina, "Well, we have peace today, you are even made mistress over me: the bishop has praised you to the skies and declared that you are freer than ever. So come and go as I do, and live your own life as you please. But don't expect any comfort or help from me."

When he had said this, his sadness grew upon him from day to day. Seeing this, Robert the dean and certain others took pity on the wretched man. And, putting their heads together to see how they could assuage his grief, they whispered in his ear a way of compelling his daughter to marry, saying, "Do you know why the bishop gave that decision the other day contrary to what was so foolishly asked of him? If you had given him money, you would certainly have won your case. Are you not aware of his greed and his vicious nature? Either of these would be sufficient; how much more when both are together! His greed will teach him to pervert justice and his vice to hate other people's virtue. When he hopes to get money from anyone's friendship, he will take that man's side. So see to it that he is on your side, and there will be no one to oppose you in the future. In order to gain your end more easily, make use of our services as your advocates." From this, Autti recovered hope and put all his cares into their hands. How astonishing is man's shamelessness, to despise the power of God and to rebel against it! But there were two reasons for this, which it may be worthwhile to give here. For when they are understood, there can be no hesitation in believing that parents can behave in this way against their own flesh and blood.

One reason, therefore, was this family's characteristic

of pursuing to the bitter end anything it had begun, whether it was good or bad, except where success was impossible. While to persevere in good is counted a virtue, to persevere in evil is the work of wickedness. Another reason was that Christina was conspicuous for such moral integrity, such comeliness and beauty, that all who knew her accounted her more lovable than all other women. Furthermore, she was so intelligent, so prudent in affairs, so efficient in carrying out her plans, that if she had given her mind to worldly pursuits she could have enriched and ennobled not only herself and her family but also all her relatives. To this was added the fact that her parents hoped she would have children who would be like her in character. So keen were they on these advantages that they begrudged her a life of virginity. For if she remained chaste for the love of Christ, they feared that they would lose her and all that they could hope to gain through her. They could not bring their minds to consider anything but the joys of the present world, thinking that anyone lacking them and seeking only invisible things would end in ruin. But we saw things turn out quite differently. For she abandoned the world and devoted herself completely as a spouse to Christ the Lord, fulfilling her resolution: while they afterward were abandoned by the world and had to take refuge with her whom they had driven out, finding with her both salvation for their souls and safety for their bodies. In this way Christina brought the hopes of her parents to naught. . . .

# HILDEGARD of BINGEN
## 1098–1179

HILDEGARD WAS a consecrated child, the youngest of ten children, given at the age of seven or eight as a kind of tithe to God, into the keeping of a relative, Jutta, who lived as an anchoress. Hildegard's parents were of noble birth, and her father, Hildebert, owned estates at Bermersheim, in Rheinhessen. Jutta's cell was set on land belonging to the Benedictine monastery of Disibodenberg, and as a group of women came to join themselves to Jutta and Hildegard, their small community became a Benedictine convent, of which Jutta was the first abbess. Closeness to the monastery gave Hildegard opportunities for learning, both academic and musical; she was particularly close to the monk Volmar, who remained a lifelong friend and wrote down many of her visions.

Hildegard took vows as a Benedictine nun when she was fifteen. When Jutta died, Hildegard, at the age of thirty-eight, was elected to take her place as abbess.

Almost from birth Hildegard had been subject to visual disturbance, seeing objects and people glowing with light, but along with this powerful sense of vision went disabling physical symptoms, probably in the form of severe migraine.

Within a few years of Jutta's death, Hildegard moved into a period of extraordinary creativity, dictating her first great visionary book, *Scivias* (an abbreviation of *Scito vias Domini,* "Know the ways of the Lord")—a collection of images illuminating theological concepts—composing a large volume of music for use in the convent, and starting an immense original scientific work in physics and medicine, which found fruit in later books. Bernard of Clairvaux, who admired her writing and thinking, recommended her to Pope Eugenius III, who became her supporter, urging her to publish her writings.

Because of the fame Hildegard brought to Disibodenberg, the abbot was shocked when Hildegard—acting, she said, on a vision—decided in 1150 to set up a new convent, independent of Disibodenberg, at Rupertsberg, some miles away. Not only the abbot but a number of the sisters as well were upset by this decision. Not all of the community followed her. One who did not was Hildegard's much-loved friend Richardis von Stade, who, against Hildegard's wishes, accepted an election as abbess at a neighboring convent. There was a tremendous tussle with Abbot Cuno to obtain a share of financial assets to set up the new foundation.

In old age Hildegard's visions told her to set off on a preaching tour, across the country she had barely seen in her sheltered life, and she traveled widely, speaking to many different kinds of audience, an extraordinary project for a woman of the period. Later she founded another community of nuns at Eibingen, near Rudesheim.

Her last years were tangled in ecclesiastical controversy, but she died peacefully in her own community.

## SCIVIAS

*Far less autobiographical writing from Hildegard exists than we might wish, but the Declaration is extraordinarily moving in setting Hildegard's life's work and genius within the context of her strange childhood and an adulthood wracked with distressing illness.*

*The visions are, in my view, the least accessible of Hildegard's writings. It is difficult to be moved either by the Ezekiel-like imagery or by the rather conventional didacticism that emerges from them, so different from, for example, Julian's transformed understanding after the Showings. It is difficult to avoid the belief that Hildegard has used vision in a literary, dramatic, and pedagogical way to convey thoughts that she particularly wishes to impress on her audience.*

### DECLARATION

THESE ARE TRUE VISIONS FLOWING FROM GOD. And behold! In the forty-third year of my earthly course, as I was gazing with great fear and trembling attention at a heavenly vision, I saw a great splendor in which resounded a voice from Heaven, saying to me:

"O fragile human, ashes of ashes, and filth of filth! Say and write what you see and hear. But since you are timid in speaking, and simple in expounding, and untaught in writing, speak and write these things not by a human mouth, and not by the understanding of human invention, and not by the requirements of human composition, but as you see and hear them on high in the heavenly places in the wonders of God. Explain these things in such a way that the hearer, receiving the words of his instructor, may expound them in those words, according to that will, vision and instruction. Thus therefore, O human, speak these things that you see and hear. And write them not by yourself or any other human being, but by the will of Him Who knows, sees, and disposes all things in the secrets of His mysteries."

And again I heard the voice from Heaven saying to me, "Speak therefore of these wonders, and, being so taught, write them and speak."

It happened that, in the eleven hundred and forty-first year of the Incarnation of the Son of God, Jesus Christ, when I was forty-two years and seven months old, Heaven was opened and a fiery light of exceeding brilliance came and permeated my whole brain and inflamed my whole heart and my whole breast, not like a burning but like a warming flame, as the sun warms anything its rays touch. And immediately I knew the meaning of the exposition of the Scriptures, namely the Psalter, the Gospel, and the other catholic volumes of both the Old and the New Testaments, though I did not have the interpretation of the words of their texts or the division of the syllables or the knowledge of cases or tenses. But I had sensed in myself wonderfully the power and mystery of secret and admirable visions from my childhood—that is, from the age of five—up to that time, as I do now. This, however, I showed to no one except a few religious persons who were living in the same manner as I; but meanwhile, until the time when God by His grace wished it to be manifested, I concealed it in quiet silence. But the visions I saw I did not perceive in dreams, or sleep, or delirium, or by the eyes of the body, or by the ears of the outer self, or in hidden places, but I received them while awake and seeing with a pure mind and the eyes and ears of the inner self, in open places, as God willed it. How this might be is hard for mortal flesh to understand.

But when I had passed out of childhood and had reached the age of full maturity mentioned above, I heard a voice from Heaven saying, "I am the Living Light, Who illuminates the darkness. The person [Hildegard] whom I have chosen and whom I have miraculously stricken as I willed, I have placed among great wonders, beyond the measure of the ancient people who saw in Me many secrets; but I have laid her low on the earth, that she might not set herself up in arrogance of mind. The world has had in her no joy or lewdness or use in worldly things, for I have withdrawn her from impudent boldness, and she feels fear and is timid in her works. For she suffers in her inmost being and in the veins of her flesh; she is distressed in mind and sense and endures great pain of body, because no security has dwelt in her, but in all her undertakings she has judged herself guilty. For I have closed up the cracks in her heart that her mind may not exalt itself in pride or vainglory but may feel fear and grief rather than joy and wantonness. Hence in My love she searched in her mind as to where she could find someone who would run in the path of salvation. And she found such a one and loved him [the monk Volmar of Disibodenberg], knowing that he was a faithful man, working like herself on another part of the work that leads to Me. And, holding fast to him, she worked with him in great zeal so that My hidden miracles might be revealed. And she did not seek to exalt herself above herself but with many sighs bowed to him whom she found in the ascent of humility and the intention of good will.

"O human, who receives these things meant to manifest what is hidden not in the disquiet of deception but in the purity of simplicity, write, therefore, the things you see and hear."

But I, though I saw and heard these things, refused to write for a long time, through doubt and bad opinion and the diversity of human words, not with stubbornness but in the exercise of humility, until, laid low by the scourge of God, I fell upon a bed of sickness; then, compelled at last by many illnesses, and by the witness of a certain noble maiden of good conduct [the nun Richardis of Stade] and of that man whom I had secretly sought and found, as mentioned above, I set my hand to the writing. While I was doing it, I sensed, as I mentioned before, the deep profundity of scriptural exposition; and, raising myself from illness by the strength I received, I brought this work to a close—though just barely—in ten years.

These visions took place and these words were written in the days of Henry, Archbishop of Mainz, and of Conrad, king of the Romans, and of Cuno, Abbott of Disibodenberg, under Pope Eugenius.

And I spoke and wrote these things not by the invention of my heart or that of any other person, but as by the secret mysteries of God I heard and received them in the heavenly places.

And again I heard a voice from Heaven saying to me, "Cry out, therefore, and write thus!"

## BOOK ONE: THE CHOIRS OF ANGELS

*Then I saw in the secret places in the heights of Heaven two armies of heavenly spirits who shone with great brightness. Those in one of the armies had on their breasts wings, with forms like human forms in front of them, on which human features showed as if in clear water. Those in the second army also had wings on their breasts, which displayed forms like human forms, in which the image of the Son of Man shone as if in a mirror. And I could see no other form either in these or in the others. These armies were arrayed in the shape of a crown around five other armies. Those in the first of these five armies seemed as if they had human forms that shone with great splendor from the shoulders down. Those in the second shone with such great brightness that I could not look at them. Those in the third had the appearance of white marble and heads like human heads, over which torches were burning, and from the shoulders down they were surrounded by an iron-gray cloud. Those in the fourth had forms like human forms and feet like human feet, and wore helmets on their heads, and marble tunics. And those in the fifth had nothing human in their appearance, and shone red like the dawn. And I saw no other form in them.*

*But these armies were also arrayed like a crown around two others. Those in the first of these other armies seemed to be full of eyes and wings, and in each eye appeared a mirror and in each mirror a human form, and they raised their wings to a celestial height. And those in the second burned like fire, and had many wings, in which they showed as if in a mirror all the Church ranks arrayed in order. And I saw no other shape either in these or in the others. And all these armies were singing with marvelous voices all kinds of music about the wonders that God works in blessed souls, and by this God was magnificently glorified.*

And I heard the voice from Heaven, saying to me:

1. GOD WONDERFULLY FORMED AND ORDERED HIS CRE-
ATION. Almighty and Ineffable God, Who was before all
ages and had no beginning and will not cease to be when
all ages are ended, marvelously by His will created every
creature and marvelously by His will set it in its place.
How? He destined some creatures to stay on the earth, but
others to inhabit the celestial regions. He also set in place
the blessed angels, both for human salvation and for the
honor of His name. How? By assigning some to help humans in their need, and others to manifest to people the
judgments of His secrets.

Therefore *you see in the secret places in the heights of
Heaven two armies of heavenly spirits who shine with
great brightness;* thus, as is shown to you in the height of
secret places that the bodily eye cannot penetrate but the
inner sight can see, these two armies indicate that the
human body and soul should serve God, since they are
going to have the brightness of eternal blessedness with the
citizens of Heaven.

2. ON THE APPEARANCE OF THE ANGELS AND ITS MEAN-
ING. *And those in one of the armies have on their breasts
wings, with forms like human forms in front of them, on
which human features show as if in clear water.* These are
the angels, who spread the desires in the depths of their
minds like wings; not that they have wings like birds, but
that in their desires they are quick to accomplish God's
will, the way a person's thoughts speed swiftly; and by
their forms they display in themselves the beauty of reason, by which God closely examines human needs; for as

a servant who hears his master's words carries them out according to his will, so the angels pay attention to God's will for humans and show Him human actions in themselves.

3. ON THE APPEARANCE OF THE ARCHANGELS AND ITS MEANING. *And so those in the second army also have wings on their breasts, which display forms like human forms, in which the image of the Son of Man shines as if in a mirror.* These are the archangels, who contemplate God's will in the desires of their intellect and display in themselves the beauty of reason; they magnify the Incarnate Word of God in the purest way, because, knowing God's secret decrees, they have often prefigured the mysteries of the Incarnation of the Son of God. *And you can see no other form either in these or in the others;* for in both the angels and the archangels there are many secret mysteries that the human intellect, weighed down by the mortal body, cannot understand. *But these armies are arrayed in the shape of a crown around five other armies.* This shows that the human body and soul must, by virtue of their strength, contain the five human senses, purify them by the five wounds of My Son, and lead them to the righteousness of governance from within.

4. ON THE APPEARANCE OF THE VIRTUES AND ITS MEANING. *And so those in the first of these five armies seem as if they have human forms that shine with great splendor from the shoulders down.* These are the Virtues, which spring up in the hearts of believers and in ardent charity build in them a lofty tower, which is their works; so that in their reason they show the deeds of the elect, and in

their strength bring them to a good end with a great glory of blessedness. How? The elect, whose inner understanding is clear, cast away all their wickedness of evil, being enlightened by these Virtues in the enlightenment of My will, and fight vigorously against the snares of the Devil; and these Virtues unceasingly show to Me their Creator these struggles against the Devil's throng. For people have within themselves struggles of confession and of denial. How? Because this one confesses Me, and that one denies Me. And in this struggle the question is: Is there a God or not? And the answer comes from the Holy Spirit Who dwells in the person: God is, and created you, and also redeemed you.

But as long as this question and answer are in a person, the power of God will not be absent from him, for this question and answer carries with it penitence. But when this question is not in a person, neither is the answer of the Holy Spirit, for such a person drives out God's gift from himself and, without the question that leads to penitence, throws himself upon death. And the Virtues display to God the battles of these wars, for they are the seal that show God the intention that worships or denies Him.

5. ON THE APPEARANCE OF THE POWERS AND ITS MEANING. *Those in the second army shine with such great brightness that you cannot look at them.* These are the Powers, and this means that no weak, mortal sinner can understand the serenity and beauty of the power of God or attain a likeness to it, for God's power is unfailing.

6. ON THE APPEARANCE OF THE PRINCIPALITIES AND ITS MEANING. *Those in the third have the appearance of white*

*marble and heads like human heads, over which torches are burning, and from the shoulders down they are surrounded by an iron-gray cloud.* These are the Principalities, and they show that those who by God's gift are rulers of people in this world must assume the true strength of justice, lest they fall into the weakness of instability. They should contemplate their Head, Who is Christ the Son of God, and direct their government according to His will for human needs, and seek the grace of the Holy Spirit in the ardor of truth, that until their end they may continue firm and unshaken in the strength of equity.

7. ON THE APPEARANCE OF THE DOMINATIONS AND ITS MEANING. *Those in the fourth have forms like human forms and feet like human feet, and wear helmets on their heads, and marble tunics.* These are the Dominations; they show that He Who is the Lord of all has raised human reason, which had lain polluted in the dust of humanity, from earth to Heaven, when He sent to earth His Son and His Son in His righteousness trod underfoot the ancient seducer; and thus the faithful should faithfully imitate Him Who is their Head, placing their hope in Heaven and fortifying themselves with the strong desire of good works.

8. ON THE APPEARANCE OF THE THRONES AND ITS MEANING. *And those in the fifth have nothing human in their appearance and shine red like the dawn.* These are the Thrones, showing that when for human salvation the Only Begotten of God, He Who was uninfected by human sin, put on a human body, Divinity bent down to humanity; for He, being conceived by the Holy Spirit in the dawn, which is to say in the Blessed Virgin, received flesh with no

spot of uncleanness whatsoever. *And you see no other form in them,* for there are many mysteries of the celestial secrets that human frailty cannot understand. *But these armies are also arrayed like a crown around two others.* This means that the faithful who direct their body's five senses to celestial things, knowing that they have been redeemed through the five wounds of the Son of God, attain with every turn and working of their mind, because they ignore the heart's pleasure and put their hope in inward things, to love of God and their neighbor.

9. ON THE APPEARANCE OF THE CHERUBIM AND ITS MEANING. *Therefore, those in the first of these other armies seem to be full of eyes and wings, and in each eye appears a mirror and in each mirror a human form, and they raise their wings to a celestial height.* These are the Cherubim, who signify knowledge of God, by which they see the mysteries of the celestial secrets and fulfill their desires according to God's will. Thus, possessing in the depth of their knowledge the purest clarity, they miraculously foresee all those who know the true God and direct their hearts' desires, like wings on which nobly and justly to arise, to Him Who is above all; and, instead of lusting after the transitory, love the eternal, as they show by the high-mindedness of their desires.

10. ON THE APPEARANCE OF THE SERAPHIM AND ITS MEANING. *And those in the second army burn like fire, and have many wings, in which they show as if in a mirror all the Church ranks arrayed in order.* These are the Seraphim, and this means that just as they burn for love of God and have the greatest desire to contemplate Him, they

also by their desires display with shining purity the ranks, both secular and spiritual, which flourish in the mysteries of the Church, for the secrets of God show wondrously in them. Therefore all who, loving sincerity with a pure heart, seek eternal life should ardently love God and embrace Him with all their will, that they may attain to the joys of those they faithfully imitate.

*But you see no other shape either in these or in the others.* This is to say that there are many secrets of the blessed spirits that are not to be shown to humans, for as long as they are mortal they cannot discern perfectly the things that are eternal.

11. ALL THESE ARMIES SING OF THE MIRACLES GOD DOES IN BLESSED SOULS. *But all these armies, as you hear, are singing with marvelous voices all kinds of music about the wonders that God works in blessed souls, by which God is magnificenty glorified.* For spirits blessed in the power of God make known in the heavenly places by indescribable sounds their great joy in the works of wonder that God perfects in His saints; by which the latter gloriously magnify God, seeking Him in the depth of sanctity and rejoicing in the joy of salvation; as My servant David, the observer of celestial secrets, testifies when he says the following things.

12. THE PSALMIST ON THIS SUBJECT. "The voice of rejoicing and of salvation in the tabernacles of the just" [Psalm 117:15]. Which is to say: The song of the gladness and joy of those who tread the flesh underfoot and lift up the spirit is known, with unfailing salvation, in the dwellings of those who reject injustice and do the works of justice;

they might do evil at the Devil's temptation, but by divine inspiration they do good. What does this mean? Man often has inappropriate exultation at committing an improperly desired sin; but in that state he does not have salvation, for he has gone against the divine command. He, however, who strongly does the good he ardently desires shall dance in the true exultation of the joy of salvation, for while in the body, he yet loves the mansion of those who run in the way of truth and turn aside from lying error.

Therefore, whoever has knowledge in the Holy Spirit and wings of faith, let this one not ignore My admonition, but taste it, embrace it, and receive it in his soul.

## BOOK TWO: CHRIST'S SACRIFICE AND THE CHURCH

76. WOMEN SHOULD NOT APPROACH THE OFFICE OF THE ALTAR. So too those of female sex should not approach the office of My altar; for they are an infirm and weak habitation, appointed to bear children and diligently nurture them. A woman conceives a child not by herself but through a man, as the ground is plowed not by itself but by a farmer. Therefore, just as the earth cannot plow itself, a woman must not be a priest and do the work of consecrating the body and blood of My Son, though she can sing the praise of her Creator, as the earth can receive rain to water its fruits. And as the earth brings forth all fruits, so in Woman the fruit of all good works is perfected. How? Because she can receive the High Priest as Bridegroom. How? A virgin betrothed to My Son will receive Him as Bridegroom, for she has shut her body away from a physical husband; and in her Bridegroom she has the

priesthood and all the ministry of My altar, and with Him possesses all its riches. And a widow too can be called a bride of My Son when she rejects a physical husband and flees beneath the wings of My Son's protection. And as a bridegroom loves his bride with exceeding love, so does My Son sweetly embrace His brides, who for love of chastity eagerly run to Him.

77. MEN AND WOMEN SHOULD NOT WEAR EACH OTHER'S CLOTHES EXCEPT IN NECESSITY. A man should never put on feminine dress or a woman use male attire, so that their roles may remain distinct, the man displaying manly strength and the woman womanly weakness; for this was so ordered by Me when the human race began. Unless a man's life or a woman's chastity is in danger; in such an hour a man may change his dress for a woman's or a woman for a man's, if they do it humbly in fear of death. And when they seek My mercy for this deed they shall find it, because they did it not in boldness but in danger of their safety. But as a woman should not wear a man's clothes, she should also not approach the office of My altar, for she should not take on a masculine role either in her hair or in her attire.

## POEMS

*Hildegard's verse is surprisingly different from her didactic writing, and it is here, as perhaps in her music, that we discover the lyrical passion of Hildegard, her ability to combine images in a way that delights and haunts the reader. Even reading her in translation it is very evident that she is a fine poet.*

*Antiphon for God the Father*

Burn everlasting one in love
as you loved when you first were
father in the burning
dawn before the world's day!

Loving your son you loved
us all into being; let us
all be his limbs.

See the need that befalls us!
Lift it away from us
and for your child's sake lead us
into safety, into bliss.

*Antiphon for the Virgin*

Because it was a woman
Who built a house for death
a shining girl tore it down.
So now
when you ask for blessings
seek the supreme one
in the form of a woman
surpassing all that God made,
since in her
(O tender! O blessed!)
he became one of us.

*Antiphon for the Virgin*

O wonder!
To a submissive
woman
the king came bowing.

This is what God did
because meekness
mounts higher than all.

"But malice flowed from woman?"
So from woman felicity
overflows.
Do you see? She makes goodness
sweeter than perfume,
brings more grace to heaven
than ever disgrace to earth.

*Alleluia verse for the Virgin*

Alleluia! light
burst from your untouched
womb like a flower
on the farther side
of death. The world-tree
is blossoming. Two
realms become one.

*Antiphon for the Creator*

Marvel at the heart
divining, at the hand
designing.

He modeled the head
of a single man—
and saw, in that globe of clay,
the world in sum.

O marvel!
God was inspired and Adam
breathed, looked
about him, lived.

*Antiphon for God the Father*

Father:
Great is our need and we beg,
we beg with a word that was
fulness within us:
look again.
It is fitting—let your word
look again that we fail not,
that your name be not
darkened within us.
Tell us your name again
lest we forget.

# The
# BEGUINES
*12th–13th centuries*

THE BEGUINES were women who, either in their own homes or in communities called Beguinages, lived lives of poverty, chastity, and prayer. Some were single, some widowed, some married but required to be celibate for as long as they remained within the Beguine movement. Some agreed to remain for a certain number of years, but all were free to leave if they wished to do so.

They were started in the middle of the twelfth century by Lambert le Begue (the Stammerer), a charismatic figure who also created the male equivalent of the Beguines, the Beghards. The Beguine movement developed at phenomenal speed, so that by the middle of the thirteenth century this way of life had spread to most European countries, enjoying particular success in the Low Countries. There were Beguine settlements in nearly every town.

The success of the Beguines had much to do with the fact that the movement offered women a new kind of opportunity. In a world where their only adult choice was between marriage and the enclosure of the convent, the Beguines supplied a third respectable alternative, a way that women could enjoy the support and companionship of other women in a stimulating spiritual and intellectual environment without taking the irrevocable step of entering a convent. The commitment of a Beguine did not preclude a later marriage.

The Beguines followed various employments—spinning, brewing, or handicrafts they could do at home. Many worked with the sick and poor, either in their own homes or in hospitals. Some Beguinages became schools where the Beguines taught neighboring children.

A later observer, John Malderus, a bishop of Antwerp in the sixteenth century, beautifully catches the unforced spirit of their lives:

> They preferred to remain chaste perpetually than to vow perpetual chastity. Likewise they were more eager to obey than to vow obedience, to cultivate poverty by frugal use of their fortunes than to abandon everything at once: they might be the kinder to the poor if something were left. They preferred to submit daily, as it were, to obedience within the enclosure than to be confined once and for all. In constant spontaneity they found compensation for perpetual claustration.*

At first the women's achievement was looked on favorably by church authorities, and there were always those, like Malderus, who found much to admire. But the wom-

---

*Quoted by Fiona Bowie in *Beguine Spirituality* (London: SPCK, 1989), 11–12.

en's relative liberty and capacity to govern themselves quite soon began to be seen as a threat to ecclesiastical control. Already in the thirteenth century doubts were being publicly expressed, and early in the fourteenth century the church took action. Several women, including Marguerite Porete, were burned, and the movement was condemned at the Council of Vienne (1311). The Beguines were accused of antinomian heresies—it was very possible to interpret their writings as saying that if you had love you did not need to bother about virtue, even though what they were actually saying was that if you had love, virtue followed naturally. Some of the women were accused, not altogether inappropriately, of belonging to a heretical movement called the Free Spirit. Some modern scholars believe the movement was invented by the accusers.

In the thirteenth century, however, persecution, though already a cloud on the horizon, was not much more than a nagging worry. It did not prevent a magnificent outpouring of religious poetry either by the Beguines or by women associated with the Beguines. The most famous of these poets are Beatrijs of Nazareth, Mechthild of Magdeburg, and Hadewijch of Brabant (or Antwerp). All of them are fascinated by the poetry of courtly love then popular, in slightly different forms, all over Europe. They had the brilliant idea of imitating the yearning ideals of the *minnesänger,* as they moped over the hopelessness of their love for "the lady," and adapting them instead to a description of the soul longing for God.

## BEATRIJS OF NAZARETH
### (ca. 1200–1268)

*Beatrijs came from a wealthy merchant family in the Brabant and began an excellent Latin education with*

*the Beguines at Zoutleeuw, which helped to shape her
later development. She went on to study at the Cistercian convent of Florival, where she received the same
education as educated boys would have received—the
trivium and the quadrivium—a study of the arts and
sciences. She later learned calligraphy and manuscript
illumination and took vows as a Cistercian. She was
to become prioress of the convent of Our Lady of
Nazareth at Lier. A scholar and intellectual by any
standard, Beatrijs was also a fine writer and poet.*

## THE POWER OF LOVE

Sometimes it happens that love is sweetly awoken in the
soul and joyfully arises and moves in the heart of itself
without us doing anything at all. And then the heart is so
powerfully touched by love, so keenly drawn into love and
so strongly seized by love, and so utterly mastered by love
and so tenderly embraced by love, that it entirely yields
itself to love. And in this it experiences a great proximity
to God, a spiritual radiance, a marvelous bliss, a noble
freedom, an ecstatic sweetness, a great overpowering by
the strength of love, and an overflowing abundance of immense delight. And then she feels that all her senses are
sanctified by love and her will has become love, and that
she is so deeply immersed and so engulfed in the abyss of
love that she herself has turned entirely into love. Then the
beauty of love has bedecked her, the power of love has
devoured her, the sweetness of love has submerged her, the
grandeur of love has consumed her, the nobility of love
has enveloped her, the purity of love has adorned her, and
the sublimity of love has drawn her upward and so united
herself with her that she always must be love and do nothing but the deeds of love.

## THE IMMENSITY OF LOVE

And so as the fish swims in the vastness of the oceans and rests in the deeps, an as the bird boldly soars in the heights and the vastness of the air, in the same way she feels her spirit roam free through the depths and the heights and the immensity of love.

## THE FAITHFULNESS OF LOVE

All those who want to attain to love must seek it with fear and pursue it with constant faithfulness, exercising an intense longing and willingly suffering without any hesitation great burdens, much pain and tribulation. They must consider every small thing to be great until they have progressed so far along the path that love reigns in them, and perfects in them her mighty works, making all things seem small, easing our toil, soothing our pain, and wiping away all the debts we owe her.

This is freedom of conscience and sweetness of heart. It is docility of mind, nobility of soul, sublimity of spirit, and the beginning of eternal life. This is to live even on earth the life of angels which is followed by life eternal, which, we pray, God in his goodness shall grant us all.

## THE DESIRE FOR GOD

The soul seeks God in his majesty; she follows him there and gazes upon him with heart and spirit. She knows him, she loves him, and she so burns with desire for him that she cannot pay heed to any saints or sinners, angels or creatures, except with that all-comprehending love of him by whom she loves all things. She has chosen him alone in love above all, beneath all, and within all, and so she desires to see God, to possess and to enjoy him with all the longing of her heart and with all the strength of her soul.

## HADEWIJCH OF BRABANT
## MID-THIRTEENTH CENTURY

*Hadewijch was an educated woman who knew French and Latin but wrote in Brabantine dialect. She was a Beguine, obviously in some position of authority in the movement, and well known as a spiritual counselor, when for some reason unknown she was disgraced.*

*Like Mechthild she used the convention of the minnesänger in her own extraordinary love poetry.*

### The Paradoxes of Love

The storming of love is what is sweetest within her,
Her deepest abyss is her most beautiful form,
To lose our way in her is to arrive,
To hunger for her is to feed and to taste,
Her despairing is sureness of faith,
Her worst wounding is to become whole again,
To waste away for her is to endure,
Her hiding is to find her at all times,
To be tormented for her is to be in good health,
In her concealment she is revealed,
What she withholds, she gives,
Her finest speech is without words,
Her imprisonment is freedom,
Her most painful blow is her sweetest consolation,
Her giving is her taking away,

Her going away is her coming near,
Her deepest silence is her highest song,
Her greatest wrath is her warmest thanks,
Her greatest threatening is remaining true,
Her sadness is the healing of all sorrow.

### *The Fury of Love*

I greet what I love
With my heart's blood
And my senses wither
In love's fury

## THE HUMANITY OF CHRIST

This is how everyone today loves themselves: they want to
live with God in consolation, in wealth, and in splendor,
and to share in the delight of his glory. We all wish to be
God with God. But, God knows, there are few enough of
us who want to live as men and women with his humanity
or to bear his cross with him, and to be crucified with him
in order to pay for the sins of the whole world. . . .

## THE SERVICE OF LOVE

Before Love breaks through and before she transports us
out of ourselves and so touches us with herself that we
become one spirit and one being with her and in her, we
must first offer her fine service and suffering: fine service
in all the works of virtue, and suffering in total obedience
to her. Thus we must stand with renewed vigor and with
hands which are ever ready for virtuous work, and with a
will that is ready for all those virtues in which Love is hon-

ored, with no other goal than that Love should take her rightful place among us and in all creatures, according to our debt to her. This is to hang on the cross with Christ, to die with him, and to rise again with him. May he always help us to this end.

## Union with God

May God make known to you, dear child, who he is and how he treats his servants and especially his handmaids, how he consumes them within himself. From the depths of his wisdom, he shall teach you what he is and with what wonderful sweetness the one lover lives in the other and so permeates the other that they do not know themselves from each other. But they possess each other in mutual delight, mouth in mouth, heart in heart, body in body, soul in soul, while a single divine nature flows through them both and they both become one through each other, yet remaining always themselves.

## Virtue Is the Measure of Love

Whoever loves God, loves his works. Now the works of God are noble virtues. Therefore, whoever loves God, loves virtue. This love is true and full of consolation. It is virtue which proves the presence of love, not sweetness of devotion, for it sometimes happens that those who love less, feel more sweetness. But it is not according to what we feel that love is measured, but according to the extent that we are grounded in charity and rooted in love.

## LEARNING PERFECTION

If you want to know this perfection, then you must first learn to know yourself in all that you do, in what you are willing to do and what you are not willing to do, in what you love and what you hate, in what you trust and what you do not trust, and in all that happens to you. You have to consider by yourself how you endure what opposes you and how you are able to go without those things which are dear to you. Of all the things that can befall a young heart, this is truly the hardest one of all: going without what we like. And when something good befalls you, examine to what use you can put it, and how wise and how moderate you are with regard to it. Try and remain inwardly detached in all that happens to you: when you are troubled or when you enjoy peace of mind. And always contemplate the works of our Lord, for these can teach you perfection.

## THE DEEPEST ESSENCE OF THE SOUL

Now understand the deepest essence of the soul: what the soul is. The soul is an essence which is transparent to God and for which God too is transparent. And the soul is more than this: it is an essence which wants to give delight to God, and which preserves its worth as long as it does not fall away to things which are alien to it and which are unworthy of it. And when the soul preserves its worth, then it becomes a groundless abyss where God is his own delight and in which he forever takes pleasure in himself in the fullest degree, as the soul does forever in him. The soul is the way that God goes when he proceeds from his depths to his liberty, that is into his ground, which is beyond the reach of all things but the soul's depths. And as long as God is not wholly her own possession, she will not be satisfied.

## LOVE'S MATURITY

In the beginning Love satisfies us,
When Love first spoke to me of love—
How I laughed at her in return!
But then she made me like the hazel trees,
Which blossom early in the season of darkness,
And bear fruit slowly.

## DRAWING CLOSE TO LOVE

I drew so close to Love
That I began to understand
How great the gain of those
Who give themselves wholly to Love:
And when I saw this for myself,
What was lacking in me gave me pain.

## MARY, MOTHER OF LOVE

Whatever gifts God bestowed upon us
There was no one who could
Understand true love
Until Mary, in her goodness,
And with deep humility,
Received the gift of Love.
She it was who tamed wild Love

And gave us a lamb for a lion;
Through her a light shone in the darkness
That had endured so long.

## MECHTHILD OF MAGDEBURG
### (CA. 1212–CA. 1282)

*Mechthild is thought to have come from a noble background, where she was versed in the intricacies of courtly love. In her late teens she left home and joined the Beguines at Magdeburg, and she remained a Beguine for about forty years. In old age, driven, it is thought, by fear of Church authorities, she entered the convent of Helfta. "Helfta was a . . . centre of Cistercian learning which had developed under the inspired leadership of Gertrude of Hackeborn, who, from the year 1251 had been abbess of the community. When Mechthild came to Helfta, Gertrude of Hackeborn was still abbess and her sister, Mechthild of Hackeborn, was mistress of the novices. In addition, Gertrude the Great, who was to be much influenced in her own work by the older Mechthild, was a child oblate of the convent. In this centre, women were able to pursue extensive studies and to develop themselves in accordance with a wealth of biblical, patristic and contemporary learning."\**

### THE CONVERSATION OF LOVE
### AND THE QUEEN

The soul drew close to love,
Greeted her reverently
And said: God greet you, Lady Love!

---

*\*Fiona Bowie, Beguine Spirituality (London: SPCK, 1989), 49.*

LOVE: May God reward you, dear Queen.

SOUL: Lady Love, you are most perfect.

LOVE: O Queen, that is why I rule all things. . . .

SOUL: Lady Love, you have taken from me all that I ever possessed on earth.

LOVE: But Lady Queen, what a blessed exchange!

SOUL: Lady Love, you took from me my childhood.

LOVE: Lady Queen, in return I give you heavenly freedom.

SOUL: Lady Love, you took from me all my youth.

LOVE: Lady Queen, in return I gave you many holy virtues.

SOUL: Lady Love, you took from me my family and my friends.

LOVE: O dear! What a pitiful lament, Lady Queen.

SOUL: Lady Love, you took from me worldly honors, worldly wealth, and the whole world.

LOVE: Lady Queen, I shall make good your loss with the Holy Spirit in a single hour, according to your wish.

SOUL: Lady Love, you overwhelmed me so completely that my body writhed in strange sickness.

LOVE: Lady Queen, in return I gave you sublime knowledge and profound thoughts.

SOUL: Lady Love, you have consumed all my flesh and blood.

LOVE: Lady Queen, you have been purified and drawn up to God.

SOUL: Lady Love, you are a thief; you must give me yet more in return.

LOVE: Lady Queen, then take me myself!

SOUL: Lady Love, now you have repaid me with a hundred-fold on earth.

LOVE: Lady Queen, now you may ask that God and all His riches be given you.

### How the Soul Speaks to God

Lord you are my lover,
My longing,
My flowing stream,
My sun,
And I am your reflection.

### How God Answers the Soul

It is my nature that makes me love you often,
For I am love itself.

It is my longing that makes me love you intensely,
For I yearn to be loved from the heart.

It is my eternity that makes me love you long,
For I have no end.

### On the Way of Suffering for God Joyfully

God leads his chosen children
Along strange paths
And it is a strange path,
And a noble path,
And a holy path
Which God himself walked:
To suffer pain without sin or guilt.

But this gives delight to the soul
Who desires God.

## The Way along Which the Soul Draws the Senses and Thus Becomes Free from Grief

It is a rare
And a high way,
Which the soul follows,
Drawing the senses after,
Just as the person with sight leads the blind.
In this way the soul is free
And lives without the heart's grief,
Desiring nothing but her Lord,
Who works all things well.

## The Wilderness Has Twelve Things

You should love what is not
And flee what is.
You should stand alone
And approach no one.
You should strive always
To be free from all things.
You should free the bound
And bind the free.
You should comfort the sick
And yet possess nothing.
You should drink the water of suffering
And feed the fire of love with the fuel of virtue.
Then you shall live in the true wilderness.

## FOUR KINDS OF HUMILITY

The first form of humility can be seen in the clothes that
we wear, which should be of an appropriate style and

clean, and in the place where we live. The second is apparent in the way that we behave towards others, whether we are loving in all circumstances and in all things. This causes the love of God to grow. The third kind of humility appears in the senses and in the way that we use and love all things rightly. The fourth form of humility lives in the soul, which is the self-effacing humility which creates so much sweet wonder in the loving soul. And it is this humility which makes us rise up to Heaven. . . .

### On the Tenfold Value of the Prayer of a Good Person

The prayer has great power
Which we pray with all our strength.
It makes an embittered heart mellow,
A sad heart joyful,
A foolish heart wise,
A timid heart bold,
A weak heart strong,
A blind heart clear-seeing,
A cold heart ardent.
It draws God who is great into a heart which is small.
It drives the hungry soul up to the fullness of God.
It unites the two lovers, God and soul, in a place of bliss,
Where they converse long of love.

### God Speaks to the Soul

And God said to the soul:
    I desired you before the world began.
    I desire you now
    As you desire me.
    And where the desires of two come together
    There love is perfected.

# CLARE
## of ASSISI
### 1196–1253

CLARE WAS BORN into a noble and wealthy family in Assisi in 1196. Her father was Favarone di Offreduccio, and
her mother Ortolana, a woman who had a reputation for
piety and for caring for the poor. Clare was noted for her
beauty, and by the time she was fifteen, her parents had
selected a suitable husband for her. But she had heard
Francis preach and arranged a secret meeting with him.
Entirely captivated by his ideas, she ran away from home
on Palm Sunday, 1212, leaving the house, according to legend, by the door used to take a corpse on its way to burial.
She was met by Francis at the Portiuncula—Saint Mary of
the Angels—where her long hair was cut off and she was
escorted by him and his friars to the local Benedictine convent until further plans could be made for her.

Clare's family made attempts to persuade her to return
home, but she refused and eventually went to live at San
Damiano, the first of the churches Francis had repaired

after his conversion. She remained there, effectively enclosed, until her death in 1253. She was joined by a number of other women, including her sister Agnes, and the sisterhood became known as the Poor Ladies of Assisi. The foundation would later be more widely known as the Poor Clares.

Francis was born of wealthy merchant stock in 1181 or 1182, and it was perhaps symbolic that the passionate friendship between himself and Clare came at a time when merchants and nobles were locked in dispute in Assisi. In his youth, Francis had lived extravagantly as a man about town, but after fighting on the side of Assisi against Perugia and enduring imprisonment, his character changed. An overwhelming conversion caused him to renounce his possessions, to identify with the poor, and to become an itinerant preacher. He drew up a simple Rule which he and his brethren—the friars—practiced, a regime of extreme poverty. Francis lived to the age of forty-four, receiving the stigmata in the last years of his life. Two years after his death he was canonized by Pope Gregory IX.

There is a good deal of reason to suppose that Francis's original plan for the Poor Ladies was that they should live a public and partly itinerant life like the friars, caring for the poor. The idea was so shocking in its time that in fact it never happened, and Clare and her sisters were given a series of Rules from Rome—six in all—that insisted on enclosure. There was real insecurity about their very existence—the Fourth Lateran Council of 1215 had forbidden the creation of new orders—and even more uncertainty about their chance to live the religious life they themselves felt appropriate to women. For Clare, even with the protection of Francis, there was, as for Héloïse in her convent at the Paraclete, the struggle with the church to be allowed to design a life suited to women, one that neither patronized them by feeling that they could not be expected to put up with hardship nor confined them by making their important decisions for them.

The relationship between Clare and Francis was a powerful one that lasted until Francis's death and, in Clare's mind, until her own death—twenty-seven years later. The extraordinary vision that had taken hold of the young girl as she heard Francis preach remained unchanged. The identification with the poverty of Jesus—with "the Babe in swaddling clothes" as she puts it, or "the Poor Crucified"—and the strange upside-down world of taking joy in having nothing continued to inspire her all her life; it is as evident in the Rule, or *forma vitae,* as she more modestly called it, that she wrote for her sisters near the end of her life as it had been in her ardent youth. She remained in some sense deeply in love with Francis and with his ideas. Yet she was no mere copy of him. Her *forma vitae* had moved some distance from his ideas about how women should live together, and her theology seems to focus most on Christ, whereas Francis emphasized the Trinity. She is "otherworldly," as he was, contrasting the shoddiness of "this world" with the glory of heaven. She used the powerful image of the "naked man" being at an advantage when it came to fighting, since there were no clothes (possessions) by which others might manipulate him.

In the twenty-seven years after Francis's death, Clare continued to rule as abbess at San Damiano. In the light of her long experience, she wrote the Rule, or *forma vitae,* printed here. While keeping faithfully to the spirit of Francis, indeed following closely the *forma vitae* he had suggested for the Poor Ladies, it introduces some important innovations—for example, it renounces the hierarchical spirit of Benedictine monasteries and convents.

The various hardships of her life—her feelings for Francis, the extreme poverty in which she lived, her struggles with Rome over a suitable Rule—may have had a bearing on the fact that she was ill for twenty-eight years, mostly confined to bed, up to the time of her death.

There are only a handful of writings that it is reasonably safe to ascribe to Clare, and they are among the earliest writing known to be by women. The Rule is one of them. The others are four letters written to Agnes, princess of Bohemia, and I have included the first of these and part of the fourth. They catch to perfection the upside-down world of Francis and Clare, in which all that makes most people happy is renounced in favor of an ecstatic inner vision that opens on a private landscape of joy. It is the privilege of the princess, Clare believes, to have refused a royal marriage to live instead in poverty and discomfort for the sake of Christ. Other writing ascribed to Clare, including the beautiful "Testament," are too doubtful to include, though I could not resist the brief "Blessing," which seems entirely in her spirit.

On the day before she died Clare received a bull, the *Solet annuere,* from Pope Innocent IV accepting her rewritten Rule in its entirety. She was delighted, and allegedly kissed it many times, no doubt feeling that it was a recognition and fruition of her life's work. Two years later, in 1255, Pope Alexander proclaimed her canonization, in the papal bull *Clara claris praeclara,* making great play with her name: "O Clare, endowed with so many titles of clarity! Clear even before your conversion, clearer in your manner of living, exceedingly clear in your enclosed life, and brilliant [clarissima] in splendor after the course of your mortal life. In Clare, a clear mirror is given to the entire world."

## THE FIRST LETTER TO
## AGNES OF PRAGUE

*Agnes, princess of Bohemia, caused public amazement when she refused to marry an emperor (possibly Frederick II), since she wished to join the Poor Ladies. For this she was publicly commended by Pope Gregory IX and received the following letter from Clare around 1234. It is written in the "noble" style. Later letters are written in the familiar style.*

To the esteemed and most holy virgin, the Lady Agnes, daughter of the most excellent and illustrious King of Bohemia: Clare, an unworthy servant of Jesus Christ and useless handmaid (cf. Luke 17:10) of the Cloistered Ladies of the Monastery of San Damiano, her subject and servant in all things, presents herself totally with a special reverent [prayer] that she attain the glory of everlasting happiness (cf. Sir. 50:5).

As I hear of the fame of Your holy conduct and irreproachable life, which is known not only to me but to the entire world as well, I greatly rejoice and exult in the Lord (Hab. 3:18). I am not alone in rejoicing at such great news, but [I am joined by] all who serve and seek to serve Jesus Christ. For, though You, more than others, could have enjoyed the magnificence and honor and dignity of the world, and could have been married to the illustrious Caesar with splendor befitting You and His Excellency. You have rejected all these things and have chosen with Your whole heart and soul a life of holy poverty and destitution. Thus You took a spouse of a more noble lineage, Who will keep Your virginity ever unspotted and unsullied, the Lord Jesus Christ:

> When You have loved [Him], You shall be chaste; when You have touched [Him], You shall become pure; when you have accepted [Him], You shall be a virgin.
> Whose power is stronger,
> Whose generosity is more abundant,
> Whose appearance more beautiful,
> Whose love more tender,
> Whose courtesy more gracious.
> In Whose embrace You are already caught up;
> Who has adorned Your breast with precious stones
>     And has placed priceless pearls in Your ears
>     and has surrounded You with sparkling gems
>     as though blossoms of springtime
>     and placed on Your head a golden crown
>     as a sign [to all] of Your holiness.

Therefore, most beloved sister, or should I say, Lady worthy of great respect: because You are the spouse and the mother and the sister of my Lord Jesus Christ (2 Cor. 11:2; Matt. 12:50), and have been adorned resplendently with the sign of inviolable virginity and most holy poverty: be strengthened in the holy service which You have undertaken out of an ardent desire for the Poor Crucified, Who for the sake of all of us took upon Himself the Passion of the Cross (Heb. 12:2) and delivered us from the power of the Prince of Darkness (Col. 1:13) to whom we were enslaved because of the disobedience of our first parent, and so reconciled us to God the Father (2 Cor. 5:18).

> O blessed poverty,
>> who bestows eternal riches on those who love and embrace her!
> O holy poverty,
>> to those who possess and desire you
>> God promises the kingdom of heaven
>> and offers, indeed, eternal glory and blessed life!
> O God-centered poverty,
>> whom the Lord Jesus Christ
>> Who ruled and now rules heaven and earth,
>> Who spoke and things were made,
>> condescended to embrace before all else!

The foxes have dens, He says, and the birds of the air have nests, but the Son of Man, Christ, has nowhere to lay His head (Matt. 8:20), but bowing His head gave up His spirit (John 19:30).

If so great and good a Lord, then, on coming into the Virgin's womb, chose to appear despised, needy, and *poor* in this world, so that people who were in utter poverty and want and in absolute need of heavenly nourishment might become rich (cf. 2 Cor. 8:9) in Him by possessing the kingdom of heaven, then rejoice and be glad (Hab. 3:18)! Be filled with a remarkable happiness and a spiritual joy! Contempt of the world has pleased You more than [its] honors, poverty more than earthly riches, and You have sought to store up greater treasures in heaven rather than on earth, where rust does not consume nor moth destroy nor thieves break in and steal (Matt. 6:20). Your reward, then, is very great in heaven (Matt. 5:12)! And You have truly merited to be called a sister, spouse, and mother (2 Cor. 11:2; Matt. 12:50) of the Son of the Father of the Most High and of the glorious Virgin.

You know, I am sure, that the kingdom of heaven is promised and given by the Lord only to the poor (cf. Matt. 5:3): for he who loves temporal things loses the fruit of love. Such a person cannot serve God and Mammon, for either the one is loved and the other hated, or the one is served and the other despised (Matt. 6:24).

You also know that one who is clothed cannot fight with another who is naked, because he is more quickly thrown who gives his adversary a chance to get hold of him; and that one who lives in the glory of earth cannot rule with Christ in heaven.

Again, [you know] that it is easier for a camel to pass through the eye of a needle than for a rich man to enter the kingdom of heaven (Matt. 19:24). Therefore, You have cast aside Your garments, that is, earthly riches, so that You might not be overcome by the one fighting against You, [and] that You might enter the kingdom of heaven through the straight path and the narrow gate (Matt. 7:13–14).

What a great laudable exchange:
> to leave the things of time for those of eternity,
> to choose the things of heaven for the goods of earth,
> to receive the hundred-fold in place of one,
> and to possess a blessed and eternal life.

Because of this I have resolved, as best I can, to beg Your excellency and Your holiness by my humble prayers in the mercy of Christ, to be strengthened in His holy service, and to progress from good to better, from virtue to virtue (Ps. 83:8), so that He Whom You serve with the total desire of Your soul may bestow on You the reward for which You long.

I also beg You in the Lord, as much as I can, to include in Your holy prayers me, Your servant, though unworthy, and the other sisters with me in the monastery, who are all devoted to You, so that by their help we may merit the mercy of Jesus Christ, and together with You may merit to enjoy the everlasting vision.

Farewell in the Lord. And pray for me.

## THE FOURTH LETTER TO
## AGNES OF PRAGUE

*This letter is believed to have been written near the time of Clare's death, at which point Agnes had spent some twenty years in religious life.*

Inasmuch as this vision is the splendor of eternal glory (Heb. 1:3), the brilliance of eternal light, and the mirror without blemish (Wis. 7:26), look upon that mirror each day, O queen and spouse of Jesus Christ, and continually study your face within it, so that you may adorn yourself within and without with beautiful robes and cover yourself with the flowers and garments of all the virtues, as becomes the daughter and most chaste bride of the Most High King. Indeed, blessed poverty, holy humility, and ineffable charity are reflected in that mirror, as, with the grace of God, you can contemplate them throughout the entire mirror.

Look at the parameters of this mirror, that is, the poverty of Him Who was placed in a manger and wrapped in swaddling clothes. O marvelous humility, O astonishing poverty! The King of the angels, the Lord of heaven and earth, is laid in a manger! Then, at the surface of the mirror, dwell on the holy humility, the blessed poverty, the untold labors and burdens which He endured for the redemption of all mankind. Then, in the depths of this same mirror, contemplate the ineffable charity which led Him to suffer on the wood of the Cross and die thereon the most shameful kind of death. Therefore, that Mirror, suspended on the wood of the Cross, urged those who passed by to consider, saying: "All you who pass by the way, look and see if there is any suffering like My suffering!" (Lam. 1:12). Let us answer Him with one voice and spirit, as He said: Remembering this over and over leaves my soul downcast within me (Lam. 3:20)! From this moment, then, O queen of our heavenly King, let yourself be inflamed more strongly with the fervor of charity!

[As you] contemplate further His ineffable delights, eternal riches and honors, and sigh for them in the great desire and love of your heart, may you cry out:

Draw me after You!
We will run in the fragrance of Your perfumes,
    O heavenly Spouse!
I will run and not tire,
    until You bring me into the wine-cellar,
    until Your left hand is under my head
    and Your right hand will embrace me happily
    [and] You will kiss me with the happiest kiss of
        Your mouth.

In this contemplation, may you remember your poor little mother, knowing that I have inscribed the happy memory of you indelibly on the tablets of my heart, holding you dearer than all the others.

What more can I say? Let the tongue of the flesh be silent when I seek to express my love for you; and let the tongue of the Spirit speak, because the love that I have for you, O blessed daughter, can never be fully expressed by the tongue of the flesh, and even what I have written is an inadequate expression.

I beg you to receive my words with kindness and devotion, seeing in them at least the motherly affection which in the fire of charity I feel daily toward you and your daughters, to whom I warmly commend myself and my daughters in Christ. On their part, these very daughters of mine, especially the most prudent virgin Agnes, our sister, recommend themselves in the Lord to you and your daughters.

Farewell, may dearest daughter, to you and to your daughters until we meet at the throne of the glory of the great God (Titus 2:13), and desire [this] for us.

Inasmuch as I can, I recommend to your charity the bearers of this letter, our dearly beloved Brother Amatus, beloved of God and men (Sir. 45:1), and Brother Bonagura. Amen.

## THE RULE OF SAINT CLARE.

*This Rule, approved by Pope Innocent IV in a bull sent to Clare on her deathbed, is the first written Rule known to be framed by a woman (though Héloïse certainly made significant additions and alterations to the Rule designed by Abelard for the Sisters of the Paraclete). Although it took its essence from Francis's teaching and suggestions for the life of the Poor Clares, Clare used her long experience after the death of Francis to work out her own ideas of what a religious community should be. Unlike the Rule of Saint Benedict, where the abbot or abbess had absolute authority, it adopts a nonhierarchical structure. The abbess has a number of experienced sisters to help her—"the discreets"—the spirit of the convent is one of consultation and consensus, not of edicts passed and obedience unwillingly exacted. Most important, the sisters are to live in as great a poverty as the men, supporting themselves by begging alms or working with their hands. To Clare, as to Héloïse, this was an assertion of women's equal strength and character, a claim that they did not need perpetual protection from men, still less the rigid control the church wished to enforce. Interestingly, the word enclosure is missing. In Clare's way of thinking it should be perfectly possible, if unusual, to leave the convent if for "some useful, reasonable, evident, and approved purpose." Like all her recommendations, it has a note of humanity, and perhaps recalls her great and perfectly reasonable need to be able to leave the enclosure of San Damiano when Francis lay dying.*

*The punishments for really recalcitrant sisters, though they may seem severe to us—the public eating of bread and water sitting on the floor—are very mild by medieval standards, where imprisonment and beating were common in religious houses. The whole emphasis of Clare's Rule is of sisterly love and sympathy, cooperation, and a measure of individual freedom to be dedicated by each sister to God.*

*Because this Rule is so revealing of the lives of medieval women religious, and of what Clare regarded as important, I have quoted it in full.*

Innocent, bishop, servant of the servants of God, to the beloved daughters in Christ the Abbess Clare and the other sisters of the Monastery of San Damiano in Assisi: our best wishes and Apostolic blessing.

The Apostolic See is accustomed to accede to the pious requests and to be favorably disposed to grant the praiseworthy desires of its petitioners. Thus, we have before Us your humble request that We confirm by [our] Apostolic authority the form of life which Blessed Francis gave you and which you have freely accepted. According to [this form of life] you are to live together in unity of mind and heart and in the profession of highest poverty. Our venerable Brother, the Bishop of Ostia and Velletri, has seen fit to approve this way of life, as the Bishop's own letters on this matter define more fully, and We have taken care to strengthen it with our Apostolic protection. Attentive, therefore, to your devout prayers, We approve and ratify what the Bishop has done in this matter and confirm it by Apostolic authority and support it by this document. To this end We include herein the text of the Bishop, which is the following:

Raynaldus, by divine mercy Bishop of Ostia and Velletri, to his most dear mother and daughter in Christ, the Lady Clare, Abbess of San Damiano in Assisi, and to her sisters, both present and to come, greetings and fatherly blessings.

Beloved daughters in Christ, because you have rejected the splendors and pleasures of the world and, *following the footprints* (1 Pet. 2:21) of Christ Himself and His most holy Mother, you have chosen to live in the cloister and to serve the Lord in highest poverty so that, in freedom of soul, you may be the Lord's servants, We approve your holy way of life in the Lord and with fatherly affection we desire freely to impart our benign favor to your wishes and holy desires. Therefore, moved by your pious prayers and by the authority of the Lord Pope as well as our own, to all of you who are now in your monastery and to all those who will succeed you We confirm forever this form of life and the manner of holy unity and highest poverty which your blessed Father Saint Francis gave you for your observance in word and writing. Furthermore, by the protection of this writing, We fortify this way of life, which is the following:

## CHAPTER 1: IN THE NAME OF THE LORD BEGINS THE FORM OF LIFE OF THE POOR SISTERS

1. The form of life of the Order of the Poor Sisters which the Blessed Francis established is this: 2. to observe the holy Gospel of our Lord Jesus Christ, by living in obedience, without anything of one's own, and in chastity.

3. Clare, the unworthy handmaid of Christ and the little plant of the most blessed Father Francis, promises obedience and reverence to the Lord Pope Innocent and to his canonically elected successors, and to the Roman Church. 4. And, just as at the beginning of her conversion, together with her sisters she promised obedience to the Blessed Francis, so now she promises his successors to observe the same [obedience] inviolably. 5. And the other sisters shall always be obliged to obey the successors of the blessed Francis and [to obey] Sister Clare and the other canonically elected Abbesses who shall succeed her.

CHAPTER II. THOSE WHO WISH TO ACCEPT THIS
LIFE AND HOW THEY ARE TO BE RECEIVED

1. If, by divine inspiration, anyone should come to us with the desire to embrace this life, the Abbess is required to seek the consent of all the sisters; and if the majority shall have agreed, having had the permission of our Lord Cardinal Protector, she can receive her. 2. And if she judges [the candidate] acceptable, let [the Abbess] carefully examine her, or have her examined, concerning the Catholic faith and the sacraments of the Church. 3. And if she believes all these things and is willing to profess them faithfully and to observe them steadfastly to the end; and if she has no husband, or if she has [a husband] who has already entered religious life with the authority of the Bishop of the diocese and has already made a vow of continence; and if there is no impediment to the observance of this life, such as advanced age or some mental or physical weakness, let the tenor of our life be clearly explained to her.

4. And if she is suitable, let the words of the holy Gospel be addressed to her: that she should *go and sell* all that she has and take care to distribute the proceeds *to the poor* (cf. Matt. 19:21). If she cannot do this, her good will suffices. 5. And let the Abbess and her sisters take care not to be concerned about her temporal affairs, so that she may freely dispose of her possessions as the Lord may inspire her. If, however, some counsel is required, let them send her to some prudent and God-fearing men, according to whose advice her goods may be distributed to the poor.

6. Afterward, once her hair has been cut off round her head and her secular dress set aside, she is to be allowed

three tunics and a mantle. 7. Thereafter, she may not go outside the monastery except for some useful, reasonable, evident, and approved purpose. 8. When the year of probation is ended, let her be received into obedience, promising to observe always our life and form of poverty.

9. During the period of probation no one is to receive the veil. 10. The sisters may also have small cloaks for convenience and propriety in serving and working. 11. Indeed, the Abbess should provide them with clothing prudently, according to the needs of each person and place, and seasons and cold climates, as it shall seem expedient to her by necessity.

12. Young girls who are received into the monastery before the age established by law should have their hair cut round [their heads]; and, laying aside their secular dress, should be clothed in religious garb as the Abbess has seen [fit]. 13. When, however, they reach the age required by law, in the same way as the others, they may make their profession. 14. The Abbess shall carefully provide a Mistress from among the more prudent sisters of the monastary both for these and the other novices. She shall form them diligently in a holy manner of living and proper behavior according to the form of our profession.

15. In the examination and reception of the sisters who serve outside the monastery, the same form as above is to be observed. 16. These sisters may wear shoes. 17. No one is to live with us in the monastery unless she has been received according to the form of our profession.

18. And for the love of the most holy and beloved Child Who *was wrapped in* the poorest of *swaddling clothes and laid in a manger* (cf. Luke 2:7–12), and of His

most holy Mother, I admonish, entreat, and exhort my sisters that they always wear the poorest of garments.

## CHAPTER III: THE DIVINE OFFICE AND FASTING, CONFESSION, AND COMMUNION

1. The Sisters who can read shall celebrate the Divine Office according to the custom of the Friars Minor; for this they may have breviaries, but they are to read it without singing. 2. And those who, for some reasonable cause, sometimes are not able to read and pray the Hours, may, like the other sisters, say the Our Father's.

3. Those who do not know how to read shall say twenty-four Our Father's for Matins; five for Lauds; for each of the hours of Prime, Terce, Sext, and None, seven; for Vespers, however, twelve; for Compline, seven. 4. For the dead, let them also say seven Our Father's with the *Requiem aeternam* in Vespers; for Matins, twelve: 5. because the sisters who can read are obliged to recite the Office of the Dead. 6. However, when a sister of our monastery shall have departed this life, they are to say fifty Our Father's.

7. The sisters are to fast at all times. 8. On Christmas, however, no matter on what day it happens to fall, they may eat twice. 9. The younger sisters, those who are weak, and those who are serving outside the monastery may be dispensed mercifully as the Abbess sees fit. 10. But in a time of evident necessity the sister are not bound to corporal fasting.

11. At least twelve times a year they shall go to confession, with the permission of the Abbess. 12. And they shall

take care not to introduce other talk unless it pertains to confession and the salvation of souls. 13. They should receive Communion seven times [a year], namely, on Christmas, and Thursday of Holy Week, Easter, Pentecost, the Assumption of the Blessed Virgin, the Feast of Saint Francis, and the Feast of All Saints. 14. [In order] to give Communion to the sisters who are in good health or to those who are ill, the Chaplain may celebrate inside [the enclosure].

## CHAPTER IV: THE ELECTION AND OFFICE OF THE ABBESS; THE CHAPTER. THOSE WHO HOLD OFFICE AND THE DISCREETS

1. In the election of the Abbess the sisters are bound to observe the canonical form. 2. However, they should arrange with haste to have present the Minister General or the Minister Provincial of the Order of Friars Minor. Through the Word of God he will dispose them to perfect harmony and to the common good in the choice they are to make. 3. And no one is to be elected who is not professed. And if a nonprofessed should be elected or otherwise given them, she is not to be obeyed unless she first professes our form of poverty.

4. At her death the election of another Abbess is to take place. 5. Likewise, if at any time it should appear to the entire body of the sisters that she is not competent for their service and common welfare, the sisters are bound to elect another as Abbess and mother as soon as possible according to the form given above.

6. The one who is elected should reflect upon the kind

of burden she has undertaken, and to Whom she is *to render an account* (Matt. 12:36) of the flock committed to her. 7. She should strive as well to preside over the others more by her virtues and holy behavior than by her office, so that, moved by her example, the sisters might obey her more out of love than out of fear. 8. She should avoid particular friendships lest by loving some more than others she cause scandal among all. 9. She should console those who are afflicted, and be, likewise, the last refuge for those who are disturbed; for, if they fail to find in her the means of health, the sickness of despair might overcome the weak.

10. She should preserve the common life in everything, especially regarding all in the church, dormitory, refectory, infirmary, and in clothing. Her vicar is bound to do likewise.

11. At least once a week the Abbess is required to call her sisters together in chapter 12. There both she and her sisters must confess their common and public offenses and negligences humbly. 13. There, too, she should consult with all her sisters on whatever concerns the welfare and good of the monastery; for the Lord often reveals what is best to the lesser [among us].

14. No heavy debt is to be incurred except with the common consent of the sisters and by reason of an evident need. This should be done through a procurator. 15. The Abbess and her sisters, however, should be careful that nothing is deposited in the monastery for safekeeping; often such practices give rise to troubles and scandals.

16. To preserve the unity of mutual love and peace, all who hold offices in the monastery should be chosen by the common consent of all the sisters. 17. And in the same

way at least eight sisters are to be elected from among the more prudent, whose counsel the Abbess is always bound to heed in those things which our form of life requires. 18. Moreover, if it seems useful and expedient, the sisters can and must sometimes depose the officials and discreets, and elect others in their place.

## CHAPTER V: SILENCE, THE PARLOR, AND THE GRILLE

1. The sisters are to keep silence from the hour of Compline until Terce, except those who are serving outside the monastery. 2. They should also keep silence continually in the church, in the dormitory, and, only while they are eating, in the refectory. 3. In the infirmary, however, they may speak discreetly at all times for the recreation and service of those who are sick. 4. However, they may briefly and quietly communicate what is really necessary always and everywhere.

5. The sisters may not speak in the parlor or at the grille without the permission of the Abbess or her Vicar. 6. And those who have permission should not dare to speak in the parlor unless they are in the presence and hearing of two sisters. 7. Moreover, they should not presume to go to the grille unless there are at least three sisters present [who have been] appointed by the Abbess or her Vicar from the eight discreets who were elected by all the sisters as the council of the Abbess. 8. The Abbess and her vicar are themselves bound to observe this custom in speaking. 9. [The sisters should speak] very rarely at the grille and, by all means, never at the door.

10. At the grille a curtain is to be hung inside which is

not to be removed except when the Word of God is being preached, or when a sister is speaking to someone. 11. The grille should also have a wooden door which is well provided with two distinct iron locks, bolts, and bars, so that, especially at night, it can be locked by two keys, one of which the Abbess is to keep and the other the sacristan; it is to be locked always except when the Divine Office is being celebrated and for reasons given above. 12. Under no circumstances whatever is any sister to speak to anyone at the grille before sunrise or after sunset. 13. Moreover, in the parlor there is always to be a curtain on the inside, which is never to be removed.

14. During the Lent of Saint Martin and the Greater Lent, no one is to speak in the parlor, except to the priest for Confession or for some other evident necessity; judgment on this is left to the prudence of the Abbess or her vicar.

## CHAPTER VI: NOT HAVING POSSESSIONS

1. After the Most High Celestial Father saw fit to enlighten my heart by His grace to do penance according to the example and teaching of our most blessed Father Saint Francis, shortly after his own conversion, I, together with my sisters, voluntarily promised him obedience.

2. When the Blessed Father saw that we had no fear of poverty, hard work, suffering, shame, or the contempt of the world, but that, instead, we regarded such things as great delights, moved by compassion he wrote for us a form of life as follows: "Since by divine inspiration you have made yourselves daughters and servants of the most

high King, the heavenly Father, and have taken the Holy Spirit as your spouse, choosing to live according to the perfection of the holy Gospel, I resolve and promise for myself and for my brothers always to have that same loving care and special solicitude for you as [I have] for them."

3. And that we might never turn aside from the most holy poverty we had embraced [nor those, either, who would come after us], shortly before his death he wrote his last will for us once more, saying: "I, brother Francis, the little one, wish to follow the life and poverty of our most high Lord Jesus Christ and of His most holy mother and to persevere in this until the end; and I ask and counsel you, my ladies, to live always in this most holy life and in poverty. And keep most careful watch that you never depart from this by reason of the teaching or advice of anyone."

4. And just as I, together with my sisters, have been ever solicitous to safeguard the holy poverty which we have promised the Lord God and the Blessed Francis, so, too, the Abbesses who shall succeed me in office and all the sisters are bound to observe it inviolably to the end: 5. that is to say, they are not to receive or hold onto any possessions or property [acquired] through an intermediary, or even anything that might reasonably be called property, 6. except as much land as necessity requires for the integrity and the proper seclusion of the monastery; and this land is not to be cultivated except as a garden for the needs of the sisters.

## Chapter VII: The Manner of Working

1. The sisters to whom the Lord has given the grace of working are to work faithfully and devotedly, [beginning]

after the Hour of Terce, at work which pertains to a virtuous life and to the common good. 2. They must do this in such a way that, while they banish idleness, the enemy of the soul, they do not extinguish the spirit of holy prayer and devotion to which all other things of our earthly existence must contribute.

3. And the Abbess or her vicar is bound to assign at the chapter, in the presence of all, the manual work each is to perform. 4. The same is to be done if alms have been sent by anyone for the needs of the sisters, so that the donors may be remembered by all in prayer together. 5. And all such things are to be distributed for the common good by the Abbess or her vicar with the advice of the discreets.

## CHAPTER VIII: THE SISTERS SHALL NOT ACQUIRE ANYTHING AS THEIR OWN; BEGGING ALMS; THE SICK SISTERS

1. The sisters shall not acquire anything as their own, neither a house nor a place nor anything at all; instead, as pilgrims and strangers in this world who serve the Lord in poverty and humility, let them send confidently for alms. 2. Nor should they feel ashamed, since the Lord made Himself poor for us in this world. This is that summit of highest poverty which has established you, my dearest sisters, as heirs and queens of the kingdom of heaven; it has made you poor in the things [of this world] but has exalted you in virtue. Let this be your portion, which leads into the land of the living (cf. Ps. 141:6). Dedicating yourselves totally to this, my most beloved sisters, do not wish to have anything else forever under heaven for the name of Our Lord Jesus Christ and His most holy Mother.

3. No sister is permitted to send letters or to receive anything or give away anything outside the monastery without the permission of the Abbess. 4. Nor is it allowed to have anything which the Abbess has not given or permitted. 5. Should anything be sent to a sister by her relatives or others, the Abbess should have it given to the sister. 6. If she needs it, the sister may use it; otherwise, let her in all charity give it to a sister who does need it. If, however, money is sent to her, the Abbess, with the advice of the discreets, may provide for the sister what she needs.

7. Regarding the sisters who are ill, the Abbess is strictly bound to inquire with all solicitude by herself and through other sisters what [these sick sisters] may need both by way of counsel and of food and other necessities, and, according to the resources of the place, she is to provide for them charitably and kindly. 8. [This is to be done] because all are obliged to serve and provide for their sisters who are ill just as they would wish to be served themselves if they were suffering from any infirmity. 9. Each should make known her needs to the other with confidence. For if a mother loves and nourishes her daughter according to the flesh, how much more lovingly must a sister love and nourish her sister according to the Spirit!

10. Those who are ill may lie on sackcloth filled with straw and may use feather pillows for their head; and those who need woolen stockings and quilts may use them.

11. When the sick sisters are visited by those who enter the monastery, they may answer them briefly, each responding with some good words to those who speak of them. 12. But the other sisters who have permission [to speak] may not dare to speak to those who enter the monastery unless [they are] in the presence and hearing of two

sister-discreets assigned by the Abbess or her vicar. 13. The Abbess and her vicar, too, are obliged themselves to observe this manner of speaking.

## CHAPTER IX: THE PENANCE TO BE IMPOSED ON THE SISTERS WHO SIN; THE SISTERS WHO SERVE OUTSIDE THE MONASTERY

1. If any sister, at the instigation of the enemy, shall have sinned mortally against the form of our profession, and if, after having been admonished two or three times by the Abbess or other sisters, she will not amend, she shall eat bread and water on the floor before all the sisters in the refectory for as many days as she has been obstinate; and if it seems advisable to the Abbess she shall undergo even greater punishment. 2. Meanwhile, as long as she remains obstinate, let her pray that the Lord will enlighten her heart to do penance. 3. The Abbess and her sisters, however, must beware not to become angry or disturbed on account of anyone's sin: for anger and disturbance prevent charity in oneself and in others.

4. If it should happen—God forbid—that through [some] word or gesture an occasion of trouble or scandal should ever arise between sister and sister, let she who was the cause of the trouble, at once, before offering the gift of her prayer to the Lord, not only prostrate herself humbly at the feet of the other and ask pardon, but also beg her earnestly to intercede for her to the Lord that He might forgive her. 5. The other sister, mindful of that word of the Lord: *If you do not forgive from the heart, neither will your* heavenly *Father forgive you* (Matt. 6:15; 18:35),

should generously pardon her sister every wrong she has done her.

6. The sisters who serve outside the monastery should not delay long outside unless some evident necessity demands it. 7. They should conduct themselves virtuously and speak little, so that those who see them may always be edified. 8. And let them zealously avoid all meetings or dealings that could be called into question. 9. They may not be godmothers of men or women lest gossip or trouble arise because of this. 10. They may not dare to repeat the rumors of the world inside the monastery. 11. And they are strictly bound not to repeat outside the monastery anything that was said or done within which could cause scandal.

12. If anyone should on occasion openly offend in these two things, it shall be left to the prudence of the Abbess to impose a penance on her with mercy. But if a sister does this through vicious habit, the Abbess, with the advice of the discreets, should impose a penance on her according to the seriousness of her guilt.

## CHAPTER X: THE ADMONITION AND CORRECTION OF THE SISTERS

1. The Abbess should admonish and visit her sisters, and humbly and charitably correct them, not commanding them anything which would be against their soul and the form of our profession. 2. The sisters, however, who are subjects, should remember that for God's sake they have renounced their own wills. Hence, they are firmly bound to obey their Abbess in all things which they promised the

Lord to observe and which are not against their soul and our profession.

3. On her part, the Abbess is to be so familiar with them that they can speak and act toward her as ladies do with their servant. For that is the way it should be, that the Abbess be the servant of all the sisters.

4. Indeed, I admonish and exhort in the Lord Jesus Christ that the sisters be on their guard against all pride, vainglory, envy, greed, worldly care and anxiety, detraction and murmuring, dissension and division. 5. Let them be ever zealous to preserve among themselves the unity of mutual love, which is the bond of perfection.

6. And those who do not know how to read should not be eager to learn. 7. Rather, let them devote themselves to what they must desire to have above all else: the Spirit of the Lord and His holy manner of working, to pray always to Him with a pure heart, and to have humility, patience in difficulty and weakness, and to love those who persecute, blame, and accuse us; for the Lord says: *Blessed are they who suffer persecution for justice's sake, for theirs is the kingdom of heaven* (Matt. 5:10). But *he who shall have persevered to the end will be saved* (Matt. 10:22).

CHAPTER XI: THE CUSTODY OF THE ENCLOSURE

1. The portress is to be mature in her manners and prudent, and of suitable age. During the day she should remain in an open cell without a door. 2. A suitable companion should be assigned to her who may, whenever necessary, take her place in all things.

3. The door is to be well secured by two different iron

locks, with bars and bolts, 4. so that, especially at night, it may be locked with two keys, one of which the portress is to have, the other the Abbess. 5. And during the day the door must not be left unguarded on any account, but should be firmly locked with one key.

6. They should take utmost care to make sure that the door is never left open, except when this can hardly be avoided gracefully. 7. And by no means shall it be opened to anyone who wishes to enter, except to those who have been granted permission by the Supreme Pontiff or by our Lord Cardinal. 8. The sisters shall not allow anyone to enter the monastery before sunrise or to remain within after sunset, unless an evident, reasonable, and unavoidable cause demands otherwise.

9. If a bishop has permission to offer mass within the enclosure, either for the blessing of an Abbess or for the consecration of one of the sisters as a nun or for any other reason, he should be satisfied with as few and virtuous companions and assistants as possible.

10. Whenever it is necessary for other men to enter the monastery to do some work, the Abbess shall carefully post a suitable person at the door who is to open it only to those assigned for the work, and to no one else. 11. At such times all the sisters should be extremely careful not to be seen by those who enter.

## CHAPTER XII: THE VISITATOR, THE CHAPLAIN, AND THE CARDINAL PROTECTOR

1. Our Visitator, according to the will and command of our Cardinal, should always be taken from the Order of

Friars Minor. 2. He should be the kind of person who is well known for his virtue and good life. 3. It shall be his duty to correct any excesses against the form of our profession, whether these be in the leadership or among the members. 4. Taking his stand in a public place, so that he can be seen by others, he may speak with several in a group and with individuals about the things that pertain to the duty of visitation, as it may seem best to him.

5. With respect for the love of God and of Blessed Francis we ask as a favor from the Order of Friars Minor a chaplain and a clerical companion of good character and reputation and prudent discretion, and two lay brothers who are lovers of holiness of life and virtue, to support us in our [life of] poverty, just as we have always had [them] through the kindness of the Order.

6. The chaplain may not be permitted to enter the monastery without his companion. 7. And when they enter, they are to remain in an open place, in such a way that they can see each other always and be seen by others. 8. For the confession of the sick who cannot go to the parlor, for their Communion, for the Last Anointing and the Prayers for the Dying, they are allowed to enter the enclosure.

9. Moreover, for funeral services and on the solemnity of Masses for the Dead, for digging or opening a grave, or also for making arrangements for it, suitable and sufficient outsiders may enter according to the prudence of the Abbess.

10. To see to all these things above, the sisters are firmly obliged to have always that Cardinal of the Holy Church of Rome as our Governor, Protector, and Corrector, who has been delegated by the Lord Pope for the Fri-

ars Minor, 11. so that, always submissive and subject at the feet of that holy Church, and steadfast in the Catholic Faith, we may observe forever the poverty and humility of our Lord Jesus Christ and of His most holy Mother and the holy Gospel which we have firmly promised. Amen.

Given at Perugia, the sixteenth day of September, in the tenth year of the Pontificate of the Lord Pope Innocent IV.

Therefore, no one is permitted to destroy this page of our confirmation or to oppose it recklessly. If anyone shall have presumed to attempt this, let him know that he will incur the wrath of Almighty God and of His holy Apostles Peter and Paul.

Given at Assisi, the ninth day of August, in the eleventh year of our Pontificate.

## THE BLESSING OF SAINT CLARE

*It is not certain that this blessing was composed, as the Poor Clare tradition has it, by the dying saint, but it certainly has her gentle style and spirit.*

In the name of the Father and of the Son and of the Holy Spirit. Amen.

May the Lord bless you and keep you. May He show His face to you and be merciful to you. May He turn His countenance to you and give you peace.

I, Clare, a handmaid of Christ, a little plant of our holy Father Francis, a sister and mother of you and the other Poor Sisters, although unworthy, ask our Lord Jesus Christ through His mercy and through the intercession of His most holy Mother Mary, of Blessed Michael the Archangel and all the holy angels of God, and of all His men and women saints, that the heavenly Father give you and confirm for you this most holy blessing in heaven and on earth. On earth, may He increase [His] grace and virtues among His servants and handmaids of His Church Militant. In heaven, may He exalt and glorify you in His Church Triumphant among all His men and women saints.

I bless you in my life and after my death as much as I can and more than I can with all the blessings with which the Father of mercies has and will have blessed His sons and daughters in heaven and on earth. Amen.

Always be lovers of God and your souls and the souls of your Sisters, and always be eager to observe what you have promised the Lord.

May the Lord be with you always and, wherever you are, may you be with Him always. Amen.

## ANGELA di FOLIGNO

### ca.1248–ca.1309

ANGELA WAS BORN in Umbria of prosperous parents. She is not thought to have had any formal schooling, but she could read and possibly write, although her *Book of the Experience of the Truly Faithful* (*Liber de vere fidelium experientia*) was, in fact, dictated. What shines out of it is her intelligence, and her extraordinary poetic gift as she attempts in vivid imagery to describe the indescribable— the interaction of God with her soul.

She married at twenty; rich and beautiful, she led a life of fashion and social pleasure. But troubled by a sin, perhaps sexual, that she felt to be mortal, she received Communion without making a confession (she was afraid to do so), knowing very well that she was not in a state of grace. As a result she was troubled by fears of damnation. When she found a confessor she could trust, and received absolution, she began what she experienced as a spiritual journey or a new life.

Umbria was full of the spirit of Saint Francis, not long dead, and Angela was influenced by his example. Gradually she gave up her expensive way of life. In a gesture reminiscent of Francis's stripping, she stood before the crucifix in the church of San Francesco, removing her clothes until she was naked. This was both an imitation of the Poverello, whom she saw as a mentor, and a sign of her throwing herself, just as she was, on God's mercy.

Her spiritual life was given a new turn when suddenly her mother, husband, and children died (presumably in an epidemic); she herself seems chillingly indifferent to this catastrophic event, telling us that she had prayed for it to happen and even describing her mother as "a great obstacle." It may be, of course, that she was denying her grief, and that her religion was part of her response to multiple loss, but she writes of the experience as a fortunate freedom from family obligations and as a sign that she was called to God's service.

She used her new freedom as a widow to sell her country estate, to give her possessions to the poor, and to embark on the life of a member of the Third Order of the Franciscans. This order of lay people wore simple gray garments and followed the example of Francis in imitating the life of the poor and suffering Christ. They cared for the poor and the sick and for lepers—people who seemed to them to be as near to Christ as possible.

Angela lived alone with one woman companion, Masazuola. She was initially very frightened at the thought of poverty, she tells us.

When she was forty-one, Angela moved into a new phase of her spiritual life, a phase full of ecstasy and alternative states of suffering and despair. It was accompanied by fits of screaming that were an embarrassment to her confessor and, at times, to Angela herself. The major aspects of her transformative experiences included her feeling caught up into the suffering of Christ and being drawn into a love relationship with him. She describes her experiences marvelously, often in the form of a dialogue between God and herself, in her *Book*.

Angela, and her thirty steps toward God, became a cult in her own lifetime, perhaps partly because of the essential joyfulness of her spirituality, despite the suffering and darkness, and partly because she did not wander as close to heresy as some other remarkable women and therefore could be recommended by clerics. There is something trustworthy and reassuring about her, even when her practices are, by modern standards extreme or, occasionally, repulsive.

## THE *BOOK* OF BLESSED ANGELA

*Angela's scribe, who describes himself as "a certain trustworthy Friar Minor," was her relative and confessor, Fra Arnaldo; he was attached at one point to the Church of Saint Francis in Assisi. He was profoundly involved in the drama of Angela's spiritual growth, and at places in the book he interrupts, in journalistic style, to tell us Angela's asides and glosses on her experience.*

*Fra Arnaldo took Angela's words down as she spoke them, in Umbrian dialect, and then translated them into Latin. He is very careful that nothing Angela feels or reports should be seen in a heretical light. In an introduction he points out that the* Book *"was*

*seen and read by the cardinal-deacon James of Co-*
*lonna . . . as well as by eight well-known lectors of*
*the Orders of Friars Minor . . . two [of them] were*
*inquisitors for many years in this Province. Moreover*
*three other friars, capable and intelligent enough to*
*be lectors, examined it, as well as many other trust-*
*worthy friars. . . . None of these saw any sign of false*
*teachings in this book."*

    *In the first extract, Angela describes a very impor-*
*tant stage in her spiritual life. "While looking at the*
*cross, I was given an even greater perception of the*
*way the Son of God . . ." In the second extract Angela*
*asks, as Julian was later to ask, to enter, so far as she*
*is capable, into the reality of the Crucifixion. Finally,*
*Fra Arnaldo asks her to tell him in detail just what it*
*is she sees in a vision of Christ, and, gifted amanuen-*
*sis that he is, he stands back from her description in*
*such a way that we can almost see and hear Angela*
*describing it to him.*

While looking at the cross, I was given an even greater
perception of the way the Son of God had died for our
sins. This perception made me aware of all my sins, and
this was extremely painful. I felt that I myself had crucified
Christ. But I still did not know which was the greatest gift
he had bestowed—whether it was the fact that he had
withdrawn me from sin and hell and converted me to the
way of penance or that he had been crucified for me.
Nonetheless, this perception of the meaning of the cross
set me so afire that, standing near the cross, I stripped myself of all my clothing and offered by whole self to him.
Although very fearful, I promised him then to maintain
perpetual chastity and not to offend him again with any of

my bodily members, accusing each of these one by one. I prayed that he himself keep me faithful to this promise, namely, to observe chastity with all the members of my body and all my senses. On the one hand, I feared to make this promise, but on the other hand, the fire of which I spoke drew it out of me, and I could not do otherwise.

In the ninth step, it was given to me to seek the way of the cross, that I too might stand at the foot of the cross where all sinners find refuge. I was instructed, illumined, and shown the way of the cross in the following manner: I was inspired with the thought that if I wanted to go to the cross, I would need to strip myself in order to be lighter and go naked to it. This would entail forgiving all who had offended me, stripping myself of everything worldly, of all attachments to men and women, of my friends and relatives and everyone else, and, likewise, of my possessions and even my very self. Then I would be free to give my heart to Christ from whom I had received so many graces, and to walk along the thorny path, that is, the path of tribulations.

I then decided to put aside my best garments, fine food, and fancy headdress. But this was still a very shameful and burdensome thing for me to do, for at this point I was not feeling any love. During this period I was still living with my husband, and it was bitter for me to put up with all the slanders and injustices leveled against me. Nonetheless, I bore these as patiently as I could. Moreover, it came to pass, God so willing, that at that time my mother, who had been a great obstacle to me, died. In like manner my husband died, as did all my sons in a short space of time. Because I had already entered the aforesaid way, and had prayed to God for their death, I felt a great consolation when it happened. I thought that since God had conceded me this aforesaid favor, my heart would always be within God's heart, and God's heart always within mine.

Once when I was meditating on the great suffering which Christ endured on the cross, I was considering the nails, which, I had heard it said, had driven a little bit of the flesh of his hands and feet into the wood. And I desired to see at least that small amount of Christ's flesh which the nails had driven into the wood. And then such was my sorrow over the pain that Christ had endured that I could no longer stand on my feet. I bent over and sat down; I stretched out my arms on the ground and inclined my head on them. Then Christ showed me his throat and his arms.

And then my former sorrow was transformed into a joy so intense that I can say nothing about it. This was a new joy, different from the others. I was so totally absorbed by this vision that I was not able to see, hear, or feel anything else. My soul saw this vision so clearly that I have no doubts about it, nor will I ever question it. I was so certain of the joy which remained in my soul that henceforth I do not believe I will ever lose this sign of God's presence. Such also was the beauty of Christ's throat or neck that I concluded that it must be divine. Through this beauty it seemed to me that I was seeing Christ's divinity, and that I was standing in the presence of God; but of that moment that is all I remember seeing. I do not know how to compare the clarity and brightness of that vision with anything or any color in the world except, perhaps, the clarity and brightness of Christ's body, which I sometimes see at the elevation of the host. . . .

When I, the brother who is writing this, heard what I believe God had wanted her to say concerning the vision of the body of Christ, I immediately noted it in my heart. Then I questioned and compelled her to tell me everything she had ever seen in this vision of the body of Christ. Under pressure from me, she began to talk: Sometimes I see the host itself just as I saw that neck or throat, and it shines with such splendor and beauty that it seems to me that it must come from God; it surpasses the splendor of the sun. This beauty which I see makes me conclude with the utmost certainty and without a shadow of a doubt that I am seeing God. When I was at home, however, the vision of Christ's neck or throat which I saw was even more beautiful, so beautiful that I believe I will never lose the joy of it. I have no way to compare it except with the vision of the host containing the body of Christ, for in the host I see a beauty which far surpasses the beauty of the sun. My soul is in great distress because I am truly unable to describe this vision.

She also told me that sometimes she sees the host in a different way, that is, she sees in it two most splendid eyes, and these are so large that it seems only the edges of the host remain visible: Once even, not in the host but in my cell, I saw the eyes and these were of such beauty and so delightful to look at that, as with the vision of the neck, I do not believe I will ever lose the joy of that vision. Though I do not know if I was asleep or awake I found myself once again in a state of great and ineffable joy, one so great that I do not believe I could ever lose it.

On another occasion she said she had seen the Christ Child in the host. He appeared to her as someone tall and very lordly, as one holding dominion. He also seemed to hold something in his hand as a sign of his dominion, and he sat on a throne: But I cannot say what he was holding

in his hands. I saw this with my bodily eyes, as I did everything I ever saw of the host. When this vision occurred I
did not kneel down like the others and I cannot recall
whether I ran right up to the altar or whether I was unable
to move because I was in such a delightful contemplative
state. I know that I was also very upset because the priest
put down the host on the altar too quickly. Christ was so
beautiful and so magnificently adorned. He looked like a
child of twelve. This vision was a source of such joy for
me that I do not believe I will ever lose the joy of it. I was
also so sure of it that I do not doubt a single detail of it.
Hence it is not necessary for you to write it. I was even so
delighted by that vision that I did not ask him to help me
nor did I have anything good or bad to say. I simply delighted in seeing that inestimable beauty.

He said: "God almighty has deposited much love in
you, more than in any woman of this city. He takes delight
in you and is fully satisfied with you and your companion.
Try to see to it that your lives are a light for all those who
wish to look upon them. A harsh judgment awaits those
who look at your lives but do not act accordingly." My
soul understood that this harsh judgment concerned the
lettered more than lay people because the former despise
these works of God though they know about them
through the Scriptures. And he went on to say: "So great
is the love that almighty God has deposited in the two of
you that he stands continually over you even if you do not
always feel his presence in the same way as you do now.
At this moment, his eyes are turned toward you." And it
did seem to me that with the eyes of the spirit I did see his
eyes and these delighted me more than I can say. I suffer

now because we speak about these things as if they were mere trifles.

Great as was my joy, I had, nonetheless, a vivid remembrance of all my sins and saw nothing good in myself. I even thought that I had never done anything pleasing to God and I remembered how much I had displeased him. As a result, I once again began to doubt that such extraordinary words had been said to me. I then went on to say: "Even if I do feel you within myself, unworthy as I am, still, if you are the Son of the almighty God, would not my soul experience an even greater joy, one greater than I could bear?" To this he replied: "I do not wish to deposit a greater joy in you than one you can presently bear. This is why it is tempered."

He had also replied: "It is true that the whole world is full of me." And then I saw that every creature was indeed full of his presence. He further added: "All things are possible for me. I can enable you to see me as I was when conversing with my disciples and yet not feel me, and I can also enable you to feel me as you feel me now and yet not see me." Even if these were not his exact words, my soul understood, nonetheless, what he was saying and even much more. I felt it was so. When I, brother scribe, interrupted to ask her: "How do you know that this is truly so?" She replied, "Because I have experienced how the soul feels it to be so."

# CATHERINE
## of SIENA
### 1347–1380

CATERINA DI GIACOMO DI BENINCASA (Catherine) was born in Siena in the period of the Black Death. She was the child of a lower-class family, the twenty-fourth of twenty-five children. Her father was a wool dyer but not poor. Unusually pious, she is said to have vowed her virginity to God at the age of seven, and she had visions and religious insights throughout her youth, as she was to do for the rest of her life. As she grew up she fell under the influence of the local Dominicans at San Domenico, where her foster brother had taken vows.

By the age of fifteen she had resolved not to marry and, in defiance of her parents' insistence that she should do so, she cut off her hair in protest. Either by parental decree or by her own choice, Catherine stayed at home after this, except to go to Mass. Legend says that she was reduced to the status of a servant by her family, and it was then that she learned to pray by withdrawing to an inner solitude;

she practiced love by treating her angry relatives as if they were the apostles. It may have been in this lonely period that she taught herself to read. At seventeen she was badly marked by smallpox, and perhaps because of this, and its effects on her chances of marriage, she succeeded in persuading her parents that she should join the Mantellate, a third-order Dominican body composed of elderly widows who did good works among the poor.

Catherine, however, continued to remain at home. When she was twenty she had a profound spiritual experience—the "mystical espousal"—after which she felt herself totally given to Christ. Like the other Mantellate, she practiced an active ministry with the sick and poor. Catherine soon gained a reputation for her kindness to the suffering; but more surprisingly for a woman, especially one who had had no formal education, she became known for her gifts as a teacher and for her skill in expounding complex theological ideas. Her mind was quick and subtle and very well informed. She became the central figure of a powerful group of thinkers who wanted to see the church reformed.

In 1370 she experienced "mystical death"—four hours of inner ecstasy but outward immobility—and she said that during this time Christ exchanged his heart for her own. She embarked on extraordinary penances amounting to virtual starvation. She was becoming increasingly in demand as a spiritual counselor and was greatly helped in her own spiritual growth by the sympathy and understanding of her confessor, Raymond of Capua. In 1374, when she was twenty-seven, another outbreak of the Black Death struck Siena, and she persuaded Raymond and others to join her in the heroic task of tending the sick and dying.

She became drawn into politics, into the conflict between the city-states and the papacy. She persuaded Pisa not to join the alliance against Pope Gregory XI, and she went to Avignon to plead the cause of the Florentines who were at odds with him. She took on larger ecclesiastical concerns—a Crusade to the Holy Land, clergy reform, the return of the papacy to Rome, which shortly took place. Everywhere she seems to have been listened to and respected, which suggests that her intelligence and spiritual authority were extraordinary. In Pisa she had received the stigmata—she had asked God that it should be invisible, and it was. She founded a convent and gained a reputation as a preacher. When she was nearly thirty, she learned to write.

A strong champion of the papacy, Catherine was summoned to Rome and lived with a group of women and men who shared her ideals. She became the confidante of those who ruled the church. She was troubled by its corruption, which she felt as a personal burden.

In the last year or two of her life she wrote what she called her book—the *Dialogue*—a debate between herself and God. The *Dialogue* is theologically derivative and impeccably orthodox and has a curiously obsessional quality as it teases out lines of thought. Catherine also wrote nearly four hundred letters in her brief adult life, some of them dictated, some personally written, many of them concerned with the state of the church.

Throughout her life Catherine had imposed severe penances on herself, including eating a very meager diet. By 1380 she was unable to eat at all, (she perceived the act of eating, perversely, as feeling "like suicide") and she gradually grew weaker and died. She was thirty-three. On October 4, 1970, Pope Paul VI made Catherine a doctor of the church, along with Teresa of Ávila.

## THE *DIALOGUE*

*In Catherine's book, perhaps the most striking image is of a bridge. One of her editors, Suzanne Noffke, suggests that the idea arose in her as a result of seeing the walled bridge with its shops spanning the Arno in Florence.*

### THE BRIDGE

*Then God eternal, to stir up even more that soul's love for the salvation of souls, responded to her:*

Before I show you what I want to show you, and what you asked to see, I want to describe the bridge for you. I have told you that it stretches from heaven to earth by reason of my having joined myself with your humanity, which I formed from the earth's clay.

This bridge, my only begotten Son, has three stairs. Two of them he built on the wood of the most holy cross, and the third even as he tasted the great bitterness of the gall and vinegar they gave him to drink. You will recognize in these three stairs three spiritual stages.

The first stair is the feet, which symbolize the affections. For just as the feet carry the body, the affections carry the soul. My Son's nailed feet are a stair by which you can climb to his side, where you will see revealed his inmost heart. For when the soul has climbed up on the feet of affection and looked with her mind's eye into my Son's opened heart, she begins to feel the love of her own heart in his consummate and unspeakable love. (I say consummate because it is not for his own good that he loves you; you cannot do him any good, since he is one with me.) Then the soul, seeing how tremendously she is loved, is herself filled to overflowing with love. So, having climbed the second stair, she reaches the third. This is his mouth, where she finds peace from the terrible war she has had to wage because of her sins.

At the first stair, lifting the feet of her affections from the earth, she stripped herself of sin. At the second she dressed herself in love for virtue. And at the third she tasted peace.

So the bridge has three stairs, and you can reach the last by climbing the first two. The last stair is so high that the flooding waters cannot strike it—for the venom of sin never touched my Son.

But though this bridge has been raised so high, it still is joined to the earth. Do you know when it was raised up? When my Son was lifted up on the wood of the most holy cross, he did not cut off his divinity from the lowly earth of your humanity. So though he was raised so high, he was not raised off the earth. In fact, his divinity is kneaded into the clay of your humanity like one bread. Nor could anyone walk on that bridge until my Son was raised up. This is why he said, "If I am lifted up high I will draw everything to myself."

When my goodness saw that you could be drawn in no other way, I sent him to be lifted onto the wood of the cross. I made of that cross an anvil where this child of humankind could be hammered into an instrument to release humankind from death and restore it to the life of grace. In this way he drew everything to himself: for he proved his unspeakable love, and the human heart is always drawn by love. He could not have shown you greater love than by giving his life for you. You can hardly resist being drawn by love, then, unless you foolishly refuse to be drawn.

I said that, having been raised up, he would draw everything to himself. This is true in two ways: First, the human heart is drawn by love, as I said, and with all its powers: memory, understanding, and will. If these three powers are harmoniously united in my name, everything else you do, in fact or in intention, will be drawn to union with me in peace through the movement of love, because all will be lifted up in the pursuit of crucified love. So my Truth indeed spoke truly when he said, "If I am lifted up high, I will draw everything to myself." For everything you do will be drawn to him when he draws your heart and its powers.

What he said is true also in the sense that everything was created for your use, to serve your needs. But you who have the gift of reason were made not for yourselves but for me, to serve me with all your heart and all your love. So when you are drawn to me, everything is drawn with you, because everything was made for you.

It was necessary, then, that this bridge be raised high. And it had to have stairs so that you would be able to mount it more easily.

This bridge has walls of stone so that travelers will not be hindered when it rains. Do you know what stones these are? They are the stones of true solid virtue. These stones were not, however, built into walls before my Son's passion. So no one could get to the final destination, even though they walked along the pathway of virtue. For heaven had not yet been unlocked with the key of my Son's blood, and the rain of justice kept anyone from crossing over.

But after these stones were hewn on the body of the Word, my gentle Son (I have told you that he is the bridge), he built them into walls, tempering the mortar with his own blood. That is, his blood was mixed into the mortar of his divinity with the strong heat of burning love.

By my power the stones of virtue were built into walls on no less a foundation than himself, for all virtue draws life from him, nor is there any virtue that has not been tested in him. So no one can have any life-giving virtue but from him, that is, by following his example and his teaching. He perfected the virtues and planted them as living stones built into walls with his blood. So now all the faithful can walk without hindrance and with no cringing fear of the rain of divine justice, because they are sheltered by the mercy that came down from heaven through the incarnation of this Son of mine.

And how was heaven opened? With the key of his blood. So, you see, the bridge has walls and a roof of mercy. And the hostelry of holy Church is there to serve the bread of life and the blood, lest the journeying pilgrims, my creatures, grow weary and faint on the way. So has my love ordained that the blood and body of my only begotten Son, wholly God and wholly human, be administered.

At the end of the bridge is the gate (which is, in fact, one with the bridge), which is the only way you can enter.

This is why he said, "I am the Way and Truth and Life; whoever walks with me walks not in darkness but in light." And in another place my Truth said that no one could come to me except through him, and such is the truth.

I explained all this to you, you will recall, because I wanted to let you see the way. So when he says that he is the Way, he is speaking the truth. And I have already shown you that he is the Way, in the image of a bridge. He says he is Truth, and so he is, and whoever follows him goes the way of truth. And he is Life. If you follow this truth you will have the life of grace and never die of hunger, for the Word has himself become your food. Nor will you ever fall into darkness, for he is the light undimmed by any falsehood. Indeed, with his truth he confounds and destroys the lie with which the devil deceived Eve. That lie broke up the road to heaven, but Truth repaired it and walled it up with his blood.

Those who follow this way are children of the truth because they follow the truth. They pass through the gate of truth and find themselves in me. And I am one with the gate and the way that is my Son, eternal Truth, a sea of peace.

But those who do not keep to this way travel below through the river—a way not of stones but of water. And since there is no restraining the water, no one can cross through it without drowning.

Such are the pleasures and conditions of the world. Those whose love and desire are not grounded on the rock but are set without order on created persons and things apart from me (and these, like water, are continually running on) run on just as they do. Though it seems to them that it is the created things they love that are running on by while they themselves remain firm, they are in fact continually running on to their end in death. They would like to preserve themselves (that is, their lives and the things they love) and not run away to nothingness. But they cannot. Either death makes them leave all behind, or by my decree these created things are taken away from them.

Such as these are following a lie by going the way of falsehood. They are children of the devil, who is the father of lies. And because they pass through the gate of falsehood they are eternally damned.

So you see, I have shown you truth and falsehood, that is, my way, which is truth, and the devil's way, which is falsehood. These are the two ways, and both are difficult.

How foolish and blind are those who choose to cross through the water when the road has been built for them! This road is such a joy for those who travel on it that it makes every bitterness sweet for them, and every burden light. Though they are in the darkness of the body, they find light, and though they are mortal, they find life without death. For through love and the light of faith they taste eternal Truth, with the promise of refreshment in return for the weariness they have borne for me. For I am grateful and sensitive. And I am just, giving each of you what you have earned: reward for good and punishment for sin.

Your tongue could never tell, nor your ears hear, nor your eyes see, the joy they have who travel on this road, for even in this life they have some foretaste of the good prepared for them in everlasting life.

They are fools indeed who scorn such a good and choose instead to taste even in this life the guarantee of hell by keeping to the way beneath the bridge. For there the going is most wearisome and there is neither refreshment nor any benefit at all, because by their sinfulness they have lost me, the supreme and eternal Good. So there is good reason—and it is my will—that you and my other servants should feel continual distress that I am so offended, as well as compassion for the harm that comes to those who so foolishly offend me.

Now you have heard and seen what this bridge is like. I have told you all this to explain what I meant when I said that my only begotten Son is a bridge, as you see he is, joining the most high with the most lowly.

# MARGERY KEMPE

---

## ca.1373–after 1439

MARGERY KEMPE was born in Bishop's Lynn (now King's Lynn) in Norfolk, England, the daughter of John Brunham, who at various times was mayor of Lynn, M.P. for the town, and coroner and justice of the peace. At the age of twenty Margery married John Kempe and almost immediately started on a wretched pregnancy of continual sickness, which was followed by a labor so grueling that she "despaired of her life." This nightmare experience perhaps tipped her into the postpartum psychosis that followed. As Margery saw it, at some time in her early adult life she had committed a grave sin (she does not say what it was), which needed absolution and which tormented her with guilt; because her confessor was both impatient and reproving, she never plucked up courage to tell him what it was she had done. Instead she fell into six months of madness, in which she heard voices and was tortured by devils. Her vision of damnation owes everything to medieval teaching about hellfire. In her suffering she reveals many symptoms that a modern psychiatrist might diagnose as paranoid schizophrenia, and even when she recovered she revealed many milder paranoid traits—being suspicious of others, constantly feeling that she was being talked about, and suffering from a general sense of being misunderstood and ill-used. The insensitivity of her confessor and other male advisers did not help. Such feelings troubled her for the rest of her life. When her psychotic illness was at its appalling height, however, she suddenly had a vision of Christ sitting lovingly at her bedside. Immediately her sanity was restored, and for the rest of her life she was to feel a special relationship to Christ and a sort of twice-born passion for her faith.

All the same, it was a long while after the healing vision before she could give up, as she felt she should, her love of expensive clothes and a general desire to make a fine appearance. No doubt they shored up her shaky self-esteem. She was helped in her extravagance by running a successful brewing business—she is the only woman in this book to have run a business and earned her own living. When the business, which went well for a time, collapsed, Margery settled fully into her religious vocation, what she calls entering the way of everlasting life. Combining this with family life brought her a good deal of neighborly disapproval, perhaps because Margery could do nothing by halves and her piety was as extreme as everything else about her. But to Margery her newfound religion remained a continuing source of happiness, giving her a strong sense of her own worth.

Margery longed to understand more of spiritual things, and she liked to haunt church dignitaries and well-known religious persons, of whom Julian was one, and discuss holy matters with them. It was a frustration to her that she could not read or write. She persuaded a literate acquaintance to read aloud to her the writings of Walter Hilton, Richard Rolle, and the Belgian Mary of Oignies. It is also possible that she knew the writing of Saint Bridget of Sweden, who, like herself, was a married woman with children, what we would call a role model.

Margery tended to feel that her religious vocation was spoiled by the fact that she was married, and she tried many times to persuade her husband, John, to agree to a life of chastity. John was a kind man, she tells us, if rather less dynamic than she would have liked, but for many years he had no intention of giving up his "rights," and Margery gave birth to fourteen children. She does not seem to think it worth mentioning them individually in her book (though she does mention one son and his German wife). Maybe many of the children died in infancy, or maybe Margery felt that, with the evidence of sexual intercourse they provide, they spoiled her image as a spiritual person. Eventually, not without difficulty, Margery persuaded John to abandon sexual intercourse, though he did so with evident reluctance.

Pilgrimages, as well as journeys to talk with famously spiritual people, became Margery's passion—she felt a tremendous need to talk and argue about her beliefs, and travel gave her a freedom that must have been unimaginable to most housewives of Lynn. She traveled to Assisi and Rome, to the Holy Land and Germany, as well as in many parts of Britain. She suffered the usual dangers of medieval travel as well as the hazard of here and there being mistaken for a Lollard. But she always managed to argue her way robustly out of danger, often telling senior clerics what she thought of them in the process.

Margery Kempe is often described with a sort of smirk by writers about mysticism who decide that even if she was not actually crazy, she was stupid and uneducated and long-windedly tiresome. It is clear that many contemporary clergy and fellow pilgrims on her travels felt much the same, exasperated by her "special relationship" with God and her capacity to release floods of tears at opportune or inopportune moments. She is about as far as she can be in temperament and manner from the reticent Julian.

Margery has naturally bad taste, a terror of being ignored, a love of sensation and drama—and particularly the drama of conflict. But she has wonderful streaks of common sense (part of her literalness), a readiness to tell us the difficult details of family life (in particular the problem of a husband who wanted more sex than she was disposed to give), and a Christian devotion that is deep and sincere.

A feminist reading of Margery not surprisingly finds her sympathetic and remarkable. She emerges as a woman of untutored intelligence, forced to live a life about which she had little choice in a society and a religion with a very low estimate of women. Her copious tears, (a common phenomenon among medieval women mystics) seem not so much mystical (though they may have been that too) as readily understandable when they are looked at in the light of how much suffering Margery's life contained, with a puerperal breakdown followed by endless painful pregnancies. Her own wish was not for more children but to pursue her own spiritual and intellectual interests, and for this she was mocked, or threatened with persecution, by neighbors and a number of clerics. Margery is more representative of the experience of women in the churches over the centuries than the great women geniuses or the cloistered female mystics. Like them she longed to be noticed and heard, to have her knowledge and insight valued, to have some life beyond being a daughter, wife, or mother. Part of what kept her going was her sense of a special relationship with Christ and his mother—they valued her, she felt, even if the world did not. She lived in a world of marvels and miracles—they were a counterweight to the pain of her woman's condition. Maybe some of the marvels that happened were a very human way of asserting her own importance, but she seemed to have a real gift for seeing into the future, which did bring her some respect.

There were a handful of people—Julian among them—who perceived the real love and longing behind Margery's questions and rambling utterances. Another who cared for her must have been the priest who took down her life story, confusing as it often is, and who preserved for the world to read the spiritual life and longing of a housewife and mother of fourteen in Bishop's Lynn.

## THE BOOKE OF MARGERY KEMPE

*Although dictated, Margery's Booke comes across with a charm and freshness that seems to capture the rich flavor of her speech. The absence of refinement and gentility makes it possible for us to learn much about the way a simple provincial woman, not a lady, thought and felt. Her religion has a thoroughgoing literalism that makes it difficult to distinguish between vision and her normal thinking; we imagine her chatting familiarly to the Virgin and Jesus as she went about her household chores. About sexual intercourse—to her it is "uncleanness"—she is also very down to earth. She doesn't want it, and John does. It does not occur to her to dress up this family crisis with euphemisms about "marital disagreement." In fact, there can rarely have been an account of a marriage as frank, or as fair, as Margery's.*

When this creature was twenty years of age, or somewhat more, she was married to a worshipful burgess [of Lynn] and was with child within a short time, as nature would have it. And after she had conceived, she was troubled with severe attacks of sickness until the child was born. And then, what with the labor pains she had in childbirth and the sickness that had gone before, she despaired of her life, believing she might not live. Then she sent for her confessor, for she had a thing on her conscience which she had never revealed before that time in all her life. For she was continually hindered by her enemy—the devil— always saying to her while she was in good health that she didn't need to confess but to do penance by herself alone, and all should be forgiven, for God is merciful enough. And therefore this creature often did great penance in fasting on bread and water, and performed other acts of charity with devout prayers, but she would not reveal that one thing in confession.

And when she was at any time sick or troubled, the devil said in her mind that she should be damned, for she was not shriven of that fault. Therefore, after her child was born, and not believing she would live, she sent for her confessor, as said before, fully wishing to be shriven of her whole lifetime, as near as she could. And when she came to the point of saying that thing which she had so long concealed, her confessor was a little too hasty and began sharply to reprove her before she had fully said what she meant, and so she would say no more in spite of anything he might do. And soon after, because of the dread she had of damnation on the one hand, and his sharp reproving of her on the other, this creature went out of her mind and was amazingly disturbed and tormented with spirits for half a year, eight weeks and odd days.

And in this time she saw, as she thought, devils opening their mouths all alight with burning flames of fire, as if they would have swallowed her in, sometimes pawing at her, sometimes threatening her, sometimes pulling her and hauling her about both night and day, during the said time. And also the devils called out to her with great threats, and bade her that she should forsake her Christian faith and belief, and deny her God, his mother, and all the saints in heaven, her good works and all good virtues, her father, her mother, and all her friends. And so she did. She slandered her husband, her friends, and her own self. She spoke many sharp and reproving words; she recognized no virtue nor goodness; she desired all wickedness; just as the spirits tempted her to say and do, so she said and did. She would have killed herself many a time as they stirred her to, and would have been damned with them in hell, and in witness of this she bit her own hand so violently that the mark could be seen for the rest of her life. And also she pitilessly tore the skin on her body near her heart with her nails, for she had no other implement, and she would have done something worse, except that she was tied up and forcibly restrained both day and night so that she could not do as she wanted.

And when she had long been troubled by these and many other temptations, so that people thought she should never have escaped from them alive, then one time as she lay by herself and her keepers were not with her, our merciful Lord Christ Jesus—ever to be trusted, worshiped be his name, never forsaking his servant in time of need—appeared to his creature who had forsaken him, in the likeness of a man, the most seemly, most beauteous, and most amiable that ever might be seen with man's eye, clad in a mantle of purple silk, sitting upon her bedside, looking upon her with so blessed a countenance that she was strengthened in all her spirits, and he said to her these words: "Daughter, why have you forsaken me, and I never forsook you?"

And as soon as he had said these words, she saw truly how the air opened as bright as any lightning, and he ascended up into the air, not hastily and quickly, but beautifully and gradually, so that she could clearly behold him in the air until it closed up again.

And presently the creature grew as calm in her wits and her reason as she ever was before, and asked her husband, as soon as he came to her, if she could have the keys of the buttery to get her food and drink as she had done before. Her maids and her keepers advised him that he should not deliver up any keys to her, for they said she would only give away such goods as there were, because she did not know what she was saying, as they believed.

Nevertheless, her husband, who always had tenderness and compassion for her, ordered that they should give her the keys. And she took food and drink as her bodily strength would allow her, and she once again recognized her friends and her household and everybody else who came to her in order to see how our Lord Jesus Christ had worked his grace in her—blessed may he be, who is ever near in tribulation. When people think he is far away from them he is very near through his grace. Afterward this creature performed all her responsibilities wisely and soberly enough, except that she did not truly know our Lord's power to draw us to him.

And when this creature had thus through grace come again to her right mind, she thought she was bound to God and that she would be his servant. Nevertheless, she would not leave her pride or her showy manner of dressing, which she had previously been used to, either for her husband or for any other person's advice. And yet she knew full well that people made many adverse comments about her, because she wore gold pipes on her head, and her hoods with the tippets were fashionably slashed. Her cloaks were also modishly slashed and underlaid with various colors between the slashes, so that she would be all the more stared at, and all the more esteemed.

And when her husband used to try to speak to her, to urge her to leave her proud ways, she answered sharply and shortly, and said that she was come of worthy kindred—he should never have married her—for her father was sometime mayor of the town of N., and afterward he was elderman of the High Guild of the Trinity in N. And therefore she would keep up the honor of her kindred, whatever anyone said.

She was enormously envious of her neighbors if they were dressed as well as she was. Her whole desire was to be respected by people. She would not learn her lesson from a single chastening experience nor be content with the worldly goods that God had sent her—as her husband was—but always craved more and more.

And then, out of pure covetousness and in order to maintain her pride, she took up brewing and was one of the greatest brewers in the town of N. for three or four years, until she lost a great deal of money, for she had never had any experience in that business. For however good her servants were and however knowledgeable in brewing, things would never go successfully for them. For when the ale had as fine a head of froth on it as anyone might see, suddenly the froth would go flat, and all the ale was lost in one brewing after another, so that her servants were ashamed and would not stay with her. Then this creature thought how God had punished her before—and she could not take heed—and now again by the loss of her goods; and then she left off and did no more brewing.

And then she asked her husband's pardon because she would not follow his advice previously, and she said that her pride and sin were the cause of all her punishing, and that she would willingly put right all her wrongdoing. But yet she did not entirely give up the world, for she now thought up a new enterprise for herself. She had a horse mill. She got herself two good horses and a man to grind people's corn, and thus she was confident of making her living. This business venture did not last long, for shortly afterward on the eve of Corpus Christi, the following marvel happened. The man was in good health, and his two horses were strong and in good condition and had drawn well in the mill previously, but now, when he took one of those horses and put him in the mill as he had done before, this horse would not pull in the mill in spite of anything the man might do. The man was sorry, and tried everything he could think of to make his horse pull. Sometimes he led him by the head, sometimes he beat him, and sometimes he made a fuss of him, but nothing did any good, for the horse would rather go backward than forward. Then this man set a pair of sharp spurs on his heels and rode on the horse's back to make him pull, but it was no better. When this man saw it was no use, he put the horse back in his stable and gave him food, and the horse ate well and freshly. And afterward he took the other horse and put him in the mill. And just as his fellow had done, so did he, for he would not pull for anything the man might do. And then this man gave up his job and would not stay any longer with the said creature.

Then it was noised about in the town of N. that neither man nor beast would serve the said creature, and some said she was accursed; some said God openly took vengeance on her; some said one thing and some said another. And some wise men, whose minds were more grounded in the love of our Lord, said it was the high mercy of our Lord Jesus Christ that called her from the pride and vanity of this wretched world.

And then this creature, seeing all these adversities coming on every side, thought they were the scourges of our Lord that would chastise her for her sin. Then she asked God for mercy, and forsook her pride, her covetousness, and the desire that she had for worldly dignity, and did great bodily penance, and began to enter the way of everlasting life as shall be told hereafter.

Another day, this creature gave herself up to meditation as she had been commanded before, and she lay still, not knowing what she might best think of. Then she said to our Lord Jesus Christ, "Jesus, what shall I think about?"

Our Lord Jesus answered in her mind, "Daughter, think of my mother, for she is the cause of all the grace that you have."

And then at once she saw Saint Anne, great with child, and then she prayed Saint Anne to let her be her maid and her servant. And presently our Lady was born, and then she busied herself to take the child to herself and look after her until she was twelve years of age, with good food and drink, with fair white clothing and white kerchiefs. And then she said to the blessed child, "My lady, you shall be the mother of God."

The blessed child answered and said, "I wish I were worthy to be the handmaiden of her that should conceive the son of God."

The creature said, "I pray you, my lady, if that grace befall you, do not discontinue with my service."

The blessed child went away for a certain time—the creature remaining still in contemplation—and afterward came back again and said, "Daughter, now I have become the mother of God."

And then the creature fell down on her knees with great reverence and great weeping and said, "I am not worthy, my lady, to do you service."

"Yes, daughter," she said, "follow me—I am well pleased with your service."

Then she went forth with our Lady and with Joseph, bearing with her a flask of wine sweetened with honey and spices. Then they went forth to Elizabeth. Saint John the Baptist's mother, and when they met together, Mary and Elizabeth reverenced each other, and so they dwelled together with great grace and gladness for twelve weeks. And then Saint John was born, and our Lady took him up from the ground with all reverence and gave him to his mother, saying of him that he would be a holy man, and blessed him.

Afterward they took leave of each other with compassionate tears. And then the creature fell down on her knees to Saint Elizabeth, and begged her that she would pray for her to our Lady so that she might still serve and please her.

"Daughter," said Elizabeth, "it seems to me that you do your duty very well."

And then the creature went forth with our Lady to Bethlehem and procured lodgings for her every night with great reverence, and our Lady was received with good cheer. She also begged for our Lady pieces of fair white cloth and kerchiefs to swaddle her son in when he was born; and when Jesus was born she arranged bedding for our Lady to lie on with her blessed son. And later she begged food for our Lady and her blessed child. Afterward she swaddled him, weeping bitter tears of compassion, mindful of the painful death that he would suffer for the love of sinful men, saying to him, "Lord, I shall treat you gently; I will not bind you tightly. I pray you not to be displeased with me."

And afterward on the twelfth day, when three kings came with their gifts and worshiped our Lord Jesus Christ in his mother's lap, this creature, our Lady's handmaiden, beholding the whole process in contemplation, wept marvelously sorely. And when she saw that they wished to take their leave to go home again to their country, she could not bear that they should go from the presence of our

Lord, and in her wonder that they wished to leave she cried so grievously that it was amazing.

And soon after, an angel came and commanded our Lady and Joseph to go from the country of Bethlehem into Egypt. Then this creature went forth with our Lady, finding her lodging day by day with great reverence, with many sweet thoughts and high meditations, and also high contemplations, sometimes continuing weeping for two hours and often longer without ceasing when in mind of our Lord's passion, sometimes for her own sin, sometimes for the sin of the people, sometimes for the souls in purgatory, sometimes for those that are in poverty or in any distress, for she wanted to comfort them all.

Sometimes she wept very abundantly and violently out of desire for the bliss of heaven, and because she was being kept from it for so long. Then this creature longed very much to be delivered out of this wretched world. Our Lord Jesus Christ said to her mind that she should remain and languish in love, "for I have ordained you to kneel before the Trinity to pray for the whole world, for many hundred thousand souls shall be saved by your prayers. And therefore, daughter, ask what you wish, and I shall grant you what you ask."

This creature said, "Lord, I ask for mercy and preservation from everlasting damnation for me and for all the world. Chastise us here as you wish and in purgatory, and of your high mercy keep us from damnation."

It happened one Friday, Midsummer Eve, in very hot weather—as this creature was coming from York carrying a bottle of beer in her hand, and her husband a cake tucked inside his clothes against his chest—that her hus-

band asked his wife this question: "Margery, if there came
a man with a sword who would strike off my head unless
I made love with you as I used to do before, tell me on
your conscience—for you say you will not lie—whether
you would allow my head to be cut off, or else allow me
to make love with you again, as I did at one time?"

"Alas, sir," she said, "why are you raising this matter,
when we have been chaste for these past eight weeks?"

"Because I want to know the truth of your heart."

And then she said with great sorrow, "Truly, I would
rather see you being killed, than that we should turn back
to our uncleanness."

And he replied, "You are no good wife."

And then she asked her husband what was the reason
that he had not made love to her for the last eight weeks,
since she lay with him every night in his bed. And he said
that he was made so afraid when he would have touched
her, that he dared do no more.

"Now, good sir, mend your ways and ask God's mercy,
for I told you nearly three years ago that you[r desire for
sex] would suddenly be slain—and this is now the third
year, and I hope yet that I shall have my wish. Good sir, I
pray you to grant what I shall ask, and I shall pray for you
to be saved through the mercy of our Lord Jesus Christ,
and you shall have more reward in heaven than if you
wore a hair shirt or wore a coat of mail as a penance. I
pray you, allow me to make a vow of chastity at whichever
bishop's hand that God wills."

"No," he said, "I won't allow you to do that, because
now I can make love to you without mortal sin, and then
I wouldn't be able to."

Then she replied, "If it be the will of the Holy Ghost

to fulfill what I have said, I pray God that you may consent to this; and if it be not the will of the Holy Ghost, I pray God that you never consent."

Then they went on toward Bridlington and the weather was extremely hot, this creature all the time having great sorrow and great fear for her chastity. And as they came by a cross her husband sat down under the cross, calling his wife to him and saying these words to her: "Margery, grant me my desire, and I shall grant you your desire. My first desire is that we shall still lie together in one bed as we have done before; the second, that you shall pay my debts before you go to Jerusalem; and the third, that you shall eat and drink with me on Fridays as you used to do."

"No, sir," she said, "I will never agree to break my Friday fast as long as I live."

"Well," he said, "then I'm going to have sex with you again."

She begged him to allow her to say her prayers, and he kindly allowed it. Then she knelt down beside a cross in the field and prayed in this way, with a great abundance of tears: "Lord God, you know all things. You know what sorrow I have had to be chaste for you in my body all these three years, and now I might have my will and I dare not, for love of you. For if I were to break that custom of fasting from meat and drink on Fridays which you commanded me, I should now have my desire. But, blessed Lord, you know I will not go against your will, and great is my sorrow now unless I find comfort in you. Now, blessed Jesus, make your will known to my unworthy self, so that I may afterward follow and fulfill it with all my might."

And then our Lord Jesus Christ with great sweetness

spoke to this creature, commanding her to go again to her husband and pray him to grant her what she desired: "And he shall have what he desires. For, my beloved daughter, this was the reason why I ordered you to fast, so that you should the sooner obtain your desire, and now it is granted to you. I no longer wish you to fast, and therefore I command you in the name of Jesus to eat and drink as your husband does."

Then this creature thanked our Lord Jesus Christ for his grace and his goodness, and afterward got up and went to her husband, saying to him, "Sir, if you please, you shall grant me my desire, and you shall have your desire. Grant me that you will not come into my bed, and I grant you that I will pay your debts before I go to Jerusalem. And make my body free to God, so that you never make any claim on me requesting any conjugal debt after this day as long as you live—and I shall eat and drink on Fridays at your bidding."

Then her husband replied to her, "May your body be as freely available to God as it has been to me."

This creature thanked God greatly, rejoicing that she had her desire, praying her husband that they should say three paternosters in worship of the Trinity for the great grace that had been granted them. And so they did, kneeling under a cross, and afterward they ate and drank together in great gladness of spirit. This was on a Friday, on Midsummer's Eve.

Then they went on to Bridlington and also to many other places, and spoke with God's servants, both anchorites and recluses, and many other of our Lord's lovers, with many worthy clerics, doctors, and bachelors of divinity as well, in many different places. And to various people among them this creature revealed her feelings and her contemplations, as she was commanded to do, to find out if there were any deception in her feelings.

And then she was commanded by our Lord to go to an anchoress in Norwich who was called Dame Julian. And so she did, and told her about the grace that God had put into her soul, of compunction, contrition, sweetness and devotion, compassion with holy meditation and high contemplation, and very many holy speeches and converse that our Lord spoke to her soul, and also many wonderful revelations, which she described to the anchoress to find out if there were any deception in them, for the anchoress was expert in such things and could give good advice.

The anchoress, hearing the marvelous goodness of our Lord, highly thanked God with all her heart for his visitation, advising this creature to be obedient to the will of our Lord and fulfill with all her might whatever he put into her soul, if it were not against the worship of God and the profit of her fellow Christians. For if it were, then it were not the influence of a good spirit, but rather of an evil spirit. "The Holy Ghost never urges a thing against charity, and if he did, he would be contrary to his own self, for he is all charity. Also he moves a soul to all chasteness, for chaste livers are called the temple of the Holy Ghost, and the Holy Ghost makes a soul stable and steadfast in the right faith and the right belief.

"And a double man in soul is always unstable and unsteadfast in all his ways. He that is forever doubting is like the wave of the sea which is moved and borne about with the wind, and that man is not likely to receive the gifts of God.

"Any creature that has these tokens may steadfastly believe that the Holy Ghost dwells in his soul. And much more, when God visits a creature with tears of contrition, devotion, or compassion, he may and ought to believe that the Holy Ghost is in his soul. Saint Paul says that the Holy Ghost asks for us with mourning and weeping unspeakable; that is to say, he causes us to ask and pray with mourning and weeping so plentifully that the tears may not be numbered. No evil spirit may give these tokens, for Saint Jerome says that tears torment the devil more than do the pains of hell. God and the devil are always at odds, and they shall never dwell together in one place, and the devil has no power in a man's soul.

"Holy Writ says that the soul of a righteous man is the seat of God, and so I trust, sister, that you are. I pray God grant you perseverance. Set all your trust in God and do not fear the talk of the world, for the more contempt, shame, and reproof that you have in this world, the more is your merit in the sight of God. Patience is necessary for you, for in that shall you keep your soul."

Great was the holy conversation that the anchoress and this creature had through talking of the love of our Lord Jesus Christ for the many days that they were together.

### JULIAN of NORWICH
1342–after 1416

JULIAN, IN HER YEARS as an anchoress, lived in an anchor-hold attached to the Church of Saint Julian at Conisford in Norwich. It is probable that her name was derived from the church—a common custom with anchoresses—and was not her original name. There is little information about Julian's personal life. She was born in 1342, but nothing is known of her parentage, whether rich or poor, or of how her family made a living. The date of her death is not known, only that it must be after 1416, since a bequest was made to her in that year—one of several Norwich wills that mention her. It is also not known at what date she entered the anchorhold—whether before or after the "Showings." Margery Kempe, in a very touching sequence in her Booke, describes going to the cell to consult her.

Julian described herself as "unlettered" and "lewd" (ignorant), but she reveals an intimate knowledge of the

Bible (the Vulgate) and of a number of spiritual classics, including the writing of Saint William of Thierry, very little of whose work, if any, had been translated from Latin into English at the time. It is possible that, like a number of other women in this book, she really could not read or write, that her knowledge of the Bible and other books came from hearing them read aloud or translated aloud, and that her "writings" were dictated, perhaps to a priest. Her intelligence, however, is so fine and clear, her interest in theological ideas so acute and profound, and her mind so disciplined as it sets out her experiences that it feels very unlikely that she would not have made the effort to learn to read, or that she had not been carefully trained in thinking and writing.

She lived in troubled times. The beginning of the Hundred Years War preceded her birth, an event with severe economic consequences in England, and was followed by several devastating epidemics of the Black Death in Norwich, together with cattle disease and severe famine. The Peasants' Revolt began in 1369, and the execution of the local leader, Geoffrey Litster, took place very near to Julian's cell.

The Great Schism (1377), and the persecution of John Wycliffe and the Lollards, occurred when Julian was in early middle age. Part of the case against the Lollards was that they wrote in English, not Latin, (though the term *Lollard* came to be used generically for those who fell out of ecclesiastical favor). Julian, who wrote in the vernacular, either from choice or because she could not write Latin, may have been risking a good deal in using her own tongue.

Nobody knows at what age Julian entered the anchorhold, whether it was before or after her great vision. Anchoresses were not uncommon in her day. With the agreement of their bishop, they made a vow not to leave their anchorhold. It might consist of one room, but quite often it consisted of two or three rooms and a garden. A servant would be kept to obtain food or other necessaries from the outside world. Strict hours of prayer would be kept, and at certain times the anchoress, sitting at a window, probably behind a curtain, would act as counselor to those needing her spiritual advice. The anchoress might practice spinning or other crafts to occupy herself and make a little money for subsistence.

The "Showings" occurred at the age of "thirty and a half," when Julian had a desperate illness. She had prayed once for such an experience—for an illness severe but not fatal so that it would enable her to identify with the sufferings of Christ, but when it came she did not appear to recognize it as the answer to her prayer, believing from the outset that she was dying. For three days she hovered between life and death; those around her certainly believed the end had come, and her curate held a crucifix up before her eyes to concentrate her thoughts on Jesus. At one point her mother, who was sitting by her, reached out to close her eyes, thinking it was all over. But Julian was to recover.

On May 8, 1373, she had what now would probably be called a near-death experience. It took the form of the now-famous revelation—the "Showings"—of Christ dying on the cross, a scene of such immediacy that it was as if she were actually there. She notes every detail of injury, pain, blood, pallor, and physical deterioration. Caught up in the horror, she enters into the agony and despair, a little as we might do in a film of Auschwitz.

Dramatically, however, at its climax the scene changes into a joyful vision of the living Christ, who talks with her and answers her questions about evil and suffering and salvation and the love of God. In the vision she sees the Virgin Mary, as she was in her perfect act of obedience at the Annunciation, again as she stood sorrowing at the cross, and then as she is in her transformation—the Mother of God. Julian also sees the devil—and smells fire and an appalling stench. This amazing experience preoccupied Julian for the rest of her life.

## THE SHOWINGS
### (SHORT TEXT)

*Soon after the vision, Julian wrote down or dictated her experiences in what is now known as the Short Text. It is included here in its entirety, both because of its unity as a piece of writing and as a contrast to the Long Text, which follows.*

# 1

Here is a vision shown by the goodness of God to a devout woman, and her name is Julian, who is a recluse at Norwich and still alive, A.D. 1413, in which vision are very many words of comfort, greatly moving for all those who desire to be Christ's lovers.

I desired three graces by the gift of God. The first was to have recollection of Christ's Passion. The second was a bodily sickness, and the third was to have, of God's gift, three wounds. As to the first, it came into my mind with devotion; it seemed to me that I had great feeling for the

Passion of Christ, but still I desired to have more by the grace of God. I thought that I wished that I had been at that time with Mary Magdalen and with the others who were Christ's lovers, so that I might have seen with my own eyes our Lord's Passion which he suffered for me, so that I might have suffered with him as others did who loved him, even though I believed firmly in all Christ's pains, as Holy Church shows and teaches, and as paintings of the Crucifixion represent, which are made by God's grace, according to Holy Church's teaching, to resemble Christ's Passion, so far as human understanding can attain. But despite all my true faith I desired a bodily sight, through which I might have more knowledge of our Lord and savior's bodily pains, and of the compassion of our Lady and of all his true lovers who were living at that time and saw his pains, for I would have been one of them and have suffered with them. I never desired any other sight of God or revelation, until my soul would be separated from the body, for I trusted truly that I would be saved. My intention was, because of that revelation, to have had truer recollection of Christ's Passion. As to the second grace, there came into my mind with contrition—a free gift from God which I did not seek—a desire of my will to have by God's gift a bodily sickness, and I wished it to be so severe that it might seem mortal, so that I should in that sickness receive all the rites which Holy Church had to give me, while I myself should believe that I was dying, and everyone who saw me would think the same, for I wanted no comfort from any human, earthly life. In this sickness I wanted to have every kind of pain, bodily and spiritual, which I should have if I were dying, every fear and assault from devils, and every other kind of pain except the departure of the spirit, for I hoped that this would be profitable to me when I should die, because I desired soon to be with my God.

I desired these two, concerning the Passion and the sickness, with a condition, because it seemed to me that neither was an ordinary petition, and therefore I said: Lord, you know what I want. If it be your will that I have it, grant it to me, and if it be not your will, good Lord, do not be displeased, for I want nothing which you do not want. When I was young I desired to have that sickness when I was thirty years old. As to the third, I heard a man of Holy Church tell the story of Saint Cecilia, and from his explanation I understood that she received three wounds in the neck from a sword, through which she suffered death. Moved by this, I conceived a great desire, and prayed our Lord God that he would grant me in the course of my life three wounds, that is, the wound of contrition, the wound of compassion, and the wound of longing with my will for God. Just as I asked for the other two conditionally, so I asked for this third without any condition. The two desires which I mentioned first passed from my mind, and the third remained there continually.

# 2

And when I was thirty and a half years old, God sent me a bodily sickness in which I lay for three days and three nights; and on the fourth night I received all the rites of Holy Church, and did not expect to live until day. But after this I suffered on for two days and two nights, and on the third night I often thought that I was on the point of death; and those who were around me also thought this. But in this I was very sorrowful and reluctant to die, not that there was anything on earth that it pleased me to live for, or anything of which I was afraid, for I trusted in God. But it was because I wanted to go on living to love God better and longer, and living so, obtain grace to know and love God more as he is in the bliss of heaven. For it seemed to me that all the time that I had lived here was very little and short in comparison with the bliss which is everlasting. So I thought: Good Lord, is it no longer to your glory that I am alive? And my reason and my sufferings told me that I should die; and with all the will of my heart I assented wholly to be as was God's will.

So I lasted until day, and by then my body was dead from the middle downward, it felt to me. Then I was moved to ask to be lifted up and supported, with cloths held to my head, so that my heart might be more free to be at God's will, and so that I could think of him while my life would last; and those who were with me sent for the parson, my curate, to be present at my end. He came with a little boy, and brought a cross; and by that time my eyes were fixed, and I could not speak. The parson set the cross before my face and said: Daughter, I have brought you the image of your savior. Look at it and take comfort from it, in reverence of him who died for you and me. It seemed to me that I was well as I was, for my eyes were set upward toward heaven, where I trusted that I was going; but nevertheless I agreed to fix my eyes on the face of the crucifix if I could, so as to hold out longer until my end came, for it seemed to me that I could hold out longer with my eyes set in front of me rather than upward. After this my sight began to fail, and it was all dark around me in the room, dark as night, except that there was ordinary light trained upon the image of the cross, I never knew how. Everything around the cross was ugly to me, as if it were occupied by a great crowd of devils.

After that I felt as if the upper part of my body were beginning to die. My hands fell down on either side, and I was so weak that my head lolled to one side. The greatest pain that I felt was my shortness of breath and the ebbing of my life. Then truly I believed that I was at the point of death. And suddenly in that moment all my pain left me, and I was as sound, particularly in the upper part of my body, as ever I was before or have been since. I was astonished by this change, for it seemed to me that it was by God's secret doing and not natural; and even so, in this ease which I felt, I had no more confidence that I should live, nor was the ease complete, for I thought that I would rather have been delivered of this world, because that was what my heart longed for.

# 3

And suddenly it came into my mind that I ought to wish for the second wound, that our Lord, of his gift and of his grace, would fill my body full with recollection and feeling of his blessed Passion, as I had prayed before, for I wished that his pains might be my pains, with compassion which would lead to longing for God. So it seemed to me that I might with his grace have his wounds, as I had wished before; but in this I never wanted any bodily vision or any kind of revelation from God, but only the compassion which I thought a loving soul could have for our Lord

Jesus, who for love was willing to become a mortal man. I desired to suffer with him, living in my mortal body, as God would give me grace. And at this, suddenly I saw the red blood trickling down from under the crown, all hot, flowing freely and copiously, a living stream, just as it seemed to me that it was at the time when the crown of thorns was thrust down upon his blessed head. Just so did he, both God and man, suffer for me. I perceived, truly and powerfully, that it was himself who showed this to me, without any intermediary; and then I said: Blessed be the Lord! This I said with a reverent intention and in a loud voice, and I was greatly astonished by this wonder and marvel, that he would so humbly be with a sinful creature living in this wretched flesh. I accepted it that at that time our Lord Jesus wanted, out of his courteous love, to show me comfort before my temptations began; for it seemed to me that I might well be tempted by devils, by God's permission and with his protection, before I died. With this sight of his blessed Passion and with his divinity, of which I speak as I understand, I saw that this was strength enough for me, yes, and for all living creatures who will be protected from all the devils of hell and from all their spiritual enemies.

# 4

And at the same time as I saw this corporeal sight, our Lord showed me a spiritual sight of his familiar love. I saw that he is to us everything which is good and comforting for our help. He is our clothing, for he is that love which wraps and enfolds us, embraces us and guides us, surrounds us for his love, which is so tender that he may never desert us. And so in this sight I saw truly that he is everything which is good, as I understand.

And in this he showed me something small, no bigger than a hazelnut, lying in the palm of my hand, and I perceived that it was as round as any ball. I looked at it and thought: What can this be? And I was given this general answer: It is everything which is made. I was amazed that it could last, for I thought that it was so little that it could suddenly fall into nothing. And I was answered in my understanding: It lasts and always will, because God loves it; and thus everything has being through the love of God.

In this little thing I saw three properties. The first is that God made it, the second is that he loves it, the third is that God preserves it. But what is that to me? It is that God is the Creator and the lover and the protector. For until I am substantially united to him, I can never have love or rest or true happiness; until, that is, I am so attached to him that there can be no created thing between my God and me. And who will do this deed? Truly, he himself, by his mercy and his grace, for he has made me for this and has blessedly restored me.

In this God brought our Lady to my understanding. I saw her spiritually in her bodily likeness, a simple, humble maiden, young in years, of the stature which she had when she conceived. Also God showed me part of the wisdom and truth of her soul, and in this I understood the reverent contemplation with which she beheld her God, marveling with great reverence that he was willing to be born of her who was a simple creature created by him. And this wisdom and truth, this knowledge of her creator's greatness and of her own created littleness, made her say meekly to the angel Gabriel: Behold me here, God's handmaiden. In this sight I saw truly that she is greater, more worthy, and more fulfilled than everything else which God has created, and which is inferior to her. Above her is no created thing, except the blessed humanity of Christ. This little thing which is created and is inferior to our Lady, Saint Mary— God showed it to me as if it had been a hazelnut—seemed to me as if it could have perished because it is so little.

In this blessed revelation God showed me three nothings, of which nothings this is the first that was shown to me. Every man and woman who wishes to live contemplatively needs to know of this, so that it may be pleasing to them to despise as nothing everything created, so as to have the love of uncreated God. For this is the reason why those who deliberately occupy themselves with earthly business, constantly seeking worldly well-being, have not God's rest in their hearts and souls; for they love and seek their rest in this thing which is so little and in which there is no rest, and do not know God who is almighty, all wise and all good, for he is true rest. God wishes to be known, and it pleases him that we should rest in him; for all things which are beneath him are not sufficient for us. And this is the reason why no soul has rest until it has despised as nothing all which is created. When the soul has become nothing for love, so as to have him who is all that is good, then is it able to receive spiritual rest.

# 5

And during the time that our Lord showed me this spiritual vision which I have now described, I saw the bodily vision of the copious bleeding of the head persist, and as long as I saw it I said, many times: Blessed be the Lord! In this first revelation of our Lord I saw in my understanding six things. The first is the tokens of his blessed Passion, and the plentiful shedding of his precious blood. The second is the virgin who is his beloved mother. The third is the blessed divinity, that always was and is and ever shall be, almighty, all wisdom, and all love. The fourth is everything which he has made; it is great and lovely and bountiful and good. But the reason why it seemed to my eyes so little was because I saw it in the presence of him who is the Creator. For to a soul who sees the Creator of all things, all that is created seems very little. The fifth is that he has made everything which is made for love, and through the same love is it preserved, and always will be without end, as has been said already. The sixth is that God is everything which is good, and the goodness which everything has is God.

This everything God showed me in the first vision, and he gave me space and time to contemplate it. And then the bodily vision ceased, and the spiritual vision persisted in my understanding, and I waited with reverent fear, rejoicing in what I saw and wishing, as much as I dared, to see more, if that were God's will, or to see for a longer time what I had already seen.

# 6

Everything that I say about myself I mean to apply to all my fellow Christians, for I am taught that this is what our Lord intends in this spiritual revelation. And therefore I pray you all for God's sake, and I counsel you for your own profit, that you disregard the wretched worm, the sinful creature to whom it was shown, and that mightily, wisely, lovingly, and meekly you contemplate God, who out of his courteous love and his endless goodness was willing to show this vision generally, to the comfort of us all. And you who hear and see this vision and this teaching, which is from Jesus Christ for the edification of your souls, it is God's will and my wish that you accept it with as much joy and delight as if Jesus had shown it to you as he did to me. I am not good because of the revelation, but only if I love God better, and so can and so should every man do who sees it and hears it with goodwill and proper intention. And so it is my desire that it should be to every man the same profit that I asked for myself, and was moved to in the first moment when I saw it; for it is common and general, just as we are all one; and I am sure that I saw it for the profit of many others. For truly it was not revealed to me because God loves me better than the humblest soul who is in a state of grace. For I am sure that there are very many who never had revelations or visions, but only the common teaching of Holy Church, who love God better than I. If I pay special attention to myself, I am nothing at all; but in general I am in the unity of love with all my fellow Christians. For it is in this unity of love that the life consists of all men who will be saved. For God is everything that is good, and God has made everything that is made, and God loves everything that he has made, and if any man or woman withdraws his love from any of his fellow Christians, he does not love at all, because he has not love toward all. And so in such times he is in danger, because he is not at peace; and anyone who has general

love for his fellow Christians has love toward everything
which is. For in mankind which will be saved is comprehended all, that is, all that is made and the maker of all;
for God is in man, and so in man is all. And he who thus
generally loves all his fellow Christians loves all, and he
who loves thus is safe. And thus will I love, and thus do I
love, and thus I am safe—I write as the representative of
my fellow Christians—and the more that I love in this way
while I am here, the more I am like the joy that I shall have
in heaven without end, that joy which is the God who out
of his endless love willed to become our brother and suffer
for us. And I am sure that anyone who sees it so will be
taught the truth and be greatly comforted, if he have need
of comfort. But God forbid that you should say or assume
that I am a teacher, for that is not and never was my intention; for I am a woman, ignorant, weak, and frail. But I
know very well that what I am saying I have received by
the revelation of him who is the sovereign teacher. But it is
truly love which moves me to tell it to you, for I want God
to be known and my fellow Christians to prosper, as I
hope to prosper myself, by hating sin more and loving God
more. But because I am a woman, ought I therefore to
believe that I should not tell you of the goodness of God,
when I saw at that same time that it is his will that it be
known? You will see this clearly in what follows, if it be
well and truly accepted. Then will you soon forget me who
am a wretch, and do this, so that I am no hindrance to
you, and you will contemplate Jesus, who is every man's
teacher. I speak of those who will be saved, for at this time
God showed me no one else; but in everything I believe as
Holy Church teaches, for I beheld the whole of his blessed
revelation of our Lord as unified in God's sight, and I

never understood anything from it which bewilders me or keeps me from the true doctrine of Holy Church.

# 7

All this blessed teaching of our Lord was shown to me in three parts, that is, by bodily vision and by words formed in my understanding and by spiritual vision. But I may not and cannot show the spiritual visions to you as plainly and fully as I should wish; but I trust in our Lord God Almighty that he will, out of his goodness and for love of you, make you accept it more spiritually and more sweetly than I can or may tell it to you, and so may it be, for we are all one in love. And in all this I was humbly moved in love toward my fellow Christians, that they might all see and know the same as I saw, for I wished it to be a comfort to them all, as it is to me; for this vision was shown for all men, and not for me alone. Of everything which I saw, this was the greatest comfort to me, that our Lord is so familiar and so courteous, and this most filled my soul with delight and surety. Then I said to the people who were with me: Today is my Doomsday. And I said this because I expected to die; because on the day that a man or a woman dies, he is judged as he will be forever. I said this because I wished them to love God more and to set less store by worldly vanity, and to make them mindful that this life is short, as they could see by my example, for in all this time I was expecting to die.

And after this I saw, in bodily vision, in the face of the crucifix which hung before me, a part of Christ's Passion: contempt, spitting to defoul his body, buffeting of his blessed face, and many woes and pains, more than I can tell; and his color often changed, and all his blessed face was for a time caked with dry blood. This I saw bodily and sorrowfully and dimly; and I wanted more of the light of day, to have seen it more clearly. And I was answered in my reason that if God wished to show me more he would, but that I needed no light but him.

# 8

And after this I saw God in an instant of time, that is, in my understanding, and by this vision I saw that he is present in all things. I contemplated it carefully, knowing and perceiving through it that he does everything which is done. I marveled at this vision with a gentle fear, and I thought: What is sin? For I saw truly that God does everything, however small it may be, and that nothing is done by chance, but it is of the endless providence of God's wisdom. Therefore I was compelled to admit that everything which is done is well done, and I was certain that God does no sin. Therefore it seemed to me that sin is nothing, for in all this sin was not shown to me. And I did not wish to go on feeling surprise at this, but I contemplated our Lord and waited for what he would show me. And on another occasion God did show me, nakedly in itself, what sin is, as I shall tell afterward.

And after this as I watched I saw the body bleeding copiously, the blood hot, flowing freely, a living stream, just as I had before seen the head bleed. And I saw this in the furrows made by the scourging, and I saw this blood run so plentifully that it seemed to me that if it had in fact been happening there, the bed and everything around it would have been soaked in blood.

God has created bountiful waters on the earth for our use and our bodily comfort, out of the tender love he has for us. But it is more pleasing to him that we accept freely his blessed blood to wash us of our sins, for there is no drink that is made which it pleases him so well to give us; for it is so plentiful, and it is of our own nature.

And after this, before God revealed any words to me, he allowed me to contemplate longer all that I had seen and all that was contained in it. And then there was formed in my soul this saying, without voice and without opening of lips: With this the fiend is overcome. Our Lord said this to me with reference to his Passion, as he had shown it to me before; and in this he brought into my mind and showed me a part of the devil's malice and all of his impotence, and this by showing me that his Passion is the overcoming of the fiend. God showed me that he still has the same malice as he had before the Incarnation, and he works as hard, and he sees as constantly as he did before that all chosen souls escape him to God's glory. And in that is all the devil's sorrow; for everything which God permits him to do turns to joy for us and to pain and shame for him, and he has as much sorrow when God permits him to work as when he is not working. And that is because he can never do as much evil as he would wish, for his power is all locked in God's hands. Also I saw our Lord scorning his malice and despising him as nothing, and he wants us to do the same. Because of this sight I laughed greatly, and that made those around me to laugh as well; and their laughter was pleasing to me. I thought that I wished that all my fellow Christians had seen what

I saw. Then they would all have laughed with me. But I did not see Christ laugh; nevertheless, it is pleasing to him that we laugh to comfort ourselves, and that we rejoice in God because the devil is overcome. And after that I became serious again, and said: I see. I see three things: sport and scorn and seriousness. I see sport, that the devil is overcome; and I see scorn, that God scorns him and he will be scorned; and I see seriousness, that he is overcome by the Passion of our Lord Jesus Christ and by his death, which was accomplished in great earnest and with heavy labor.

After this our Lord said: I thank you for your service and your labor, and especially in your youth.

# 9

God showed me three degrees of bliss that every soul will have in heaven who has voluntarily served God in any degree here upon earth. The first is the honor of the thanks of our Lord God which he will receive when he is delivered from pain. This thanks is so exalted and so honorable that it will seem to him that this suffices him, if there were no other happiness. For it seemed to me that all the pain and labor which all living men might endure could not earn the thanks that one man will have who has voluntarily served God. As to the second degree, it is that all the blessed in heaven will see the honor of the thanks from our Lord God. This makes a soul's service known to all who are in heaven. And for the third degree, which is that the first joy with which the soul is then received will last forevermore, I saw that this was kindly and sweetly said and revealed to me: Every man's age will be known in heaven, and he will be rewarded for his voluntary service and for the time he has served; and especially the age of those who voluntarily and freely offer their youth to God is fittingly rewarded and wonderfully thanked.

And after this our Lord revealed to me a supreme spiritual delight in my soul. In this delight I was filled full of everlasting surety, and I was powerfully secured without any fear. This sensation was so welcome and so dear to me that I was at peace, at ease and at rest, so that there was nothing upon earth which could have afflicted me.

This lasted only for a time, and then I was changed, and left to myself, oppressed and weary of myself, ruing my life so that I scarcely had the patience to go on living. I felt that there was no ease or comfort for me except hope, faith, and love, and truly I felt very little of this. And then presently God gave me again comfort and rest for my soul, delight and security so blessed and so powerful that there was no fear, no sorrow, no pain, physical or spiritual, that one could suffer which might have disturbed me. And then again I felt the pain, and then afterward the joy and the delight, now the one and now the other, again and again, I suppose about twenty times. And in the time of joy I could have said with Paul: Nothing shall separate me from the love of Christ; and in the pain, I could have said with Peter: Lord, save me, I am perishing.

This vision was shown to me to teach me to understand that every man needs to experience this, to be comforted at one time, and at another to fail and to be left to himself. God wishes us to know that he keeps us safe all the time, in joy and in sorrow, and that he loves us as much in sorrow as in joy. And sometimes a man is left to himself for the profit of his soul, and neither the one nor the other is caused by sin. For in this time I committed no sin for which I ought to have been left to myself, nor did I deserve these sensations of joy; but God gives joy freely as it pleases him, and sometimes he allows us to be in sorrow, and both come from his love. For it is God's will that we do all in our power to preserve our consolation, for bliss lasts forevermore, and pain is passing and will be reduced to nothing. Therefore it is not God's will that when we feel pain we should pursue it, sorrowing and mourning for it, but that suddenly we should pass it over and preserve ourselves in endless delight, because God is almighty, our lover and preserver.

# 10

After this Christ showed me part of his Passion, close to his death. I saw his sweet face as it were dry and bloodless, with the pallor of dying, then more dead, pale and languishing, then the pallor turning blue and then more blue, as death took more hold upon his flesh. For all the pains which Christ suffered in his body appeared to me in his blessed face, in all that I could see of it, and especially in the lips. I saw there what had become of the four colors that I had seen before, his freshness, his ruddiness, his vitality, and his beauty which I had seen. This was a grievous change to watch, this deep dying, and the nose shriveled and dried up as I saw. The long torment seemed to me as if he had been dead for a week and had still gone on suffering pain, and it seemed to me as if the greatest and the last pain of his Passion was when his flesh dried up. And in this drying what Christ had said came to my mind: I thirst. For I saw in Christ a double thirst, one physical, the other spiritual. This saying was shown to me to signify the physical thirst, and what was revealed to me of the spiritual thirst I shall say afterward; and concerning the physical thirst, I understood that the body was wholly dried up, for his blessed flesh and bones were left without blood or moisture. The blessed body was left to dry for a long time, with the wrenching of the nails and the sagging of the head and the weight of the body, with the blowing of the wind around him, which dried up his body and pained him with cold, more than my heart can think of, and with all his other pains I saw such pain that all that I can describe or say is inadequate, for it cannot be described. But each soul should do as Saint Paul says, and feel in himself what is in Christ Jesus. This revelation of Christ's pains filled me full of pains, for I know well that he suffered only once, but it was now his will to show it to me and fill me with its recollection, as I had asked before. My mother, who was standing there with the others, held up her hand in front of my face to close my eyes, for she thought that I was already dead or had that moment died; and this greatly increased my sorrow, for despite all my pains, I did not want to be hindered from seeing, because of my love for him. And with regard to either, in all this time that Christ was present to me, I felt no pain except for Christ's pains; and then it came to me that I had little known what pain it was that I had asked for, for it seemed to me that my pains exceeded any mortal death. I thought: Is there any pain in hell like this? And in my reason I was answered that despair is greater, for that is a spiritual pain. But there is no greater physical pain than this; how could I suffer greater pain than to see him who is all my life, all my bliss, and all my joy suffer? Here I felt truly that I loved Christ so much more than myself that I thought it would have been a great comfort to me if my body had died.

In this I saw part of the compassion of our Lady, Saint Mary, for Christ and she were so united in love that the greatness of her love was the cause of the greatness of her pain. For her pain surpassed that of all others, as much as she loved him more than all others. And so all his disciples and all his true lovers suffered greater pains than they did at the death of their own bodies. For I am sure, by my own experience, that the least of them loved him more than they loved themselves. And here I saw a great unity between Christ and us; for when he was in pain we were in pain, and all creatures able to suffer pain suffered with him. And for those that did not know him, their pain was that all creation, sun and moon, ceased to serve men, and so they were all abandoned in sorrow at that time. So those who loved him suffered pain for their love, and those who did not love him suffered pain because the comfort of all creation failed them.

At this time I wanted to look to the side of the cross, but I did not dare, for I knew well that while I looked at the cross I was secure and safe. Therefore I would not agree to put my soul in danger, for apart from the cross there was no safety, but only the horror of devils.

Then there came a suggestion, seemingly friendly, to my reason. It was said to me: Look up to heaven to his Father. Then I saw clearly by the faith which I felt that there was nothing between the cross and heaven which could have grieved me, and that I must either look up or else answer. I answered, and said: No, I cannot, for you are my heaven. I said this because I did not want to look up, for I would rather have remained in that pain until Judgment Day than have come to heaven any other way than by him. For I knew well that he who had bought me so dearly would unbind me when it was his will.

# 11

Thus I chose Jesus for my heaven, whom I saw only in pain at that time. No other heaven was pleasing to me than Jesus, who will be my bliss when I am there; and this has always been a comfort to me, that I chose Jesus as my heaven in all times of suffering and of sorrow. And that has taught me that I should always do so, and choose only him to be my heaven in well-being and in woe. And so I saw my Lord Jesus languishing for long, because of the union in him of man and God, for love gave strength to his humanity to suffer more than all men could. I mean not only more pain than any other one man could suffer, but also that he suffered more pain than would all men together, from the first beginning to the last day. No tongue may tell, no heart can fully think of the pains which our savior suffered for us, if we have regard to the honor of him who is the highest, most majestic king, and to his shameful, grievous, and painful death. For he who was highest and most honorable was most completely brought low, most utterly despised. But the love which made him suffer all this surpasses all his pains as far as heaven is above earth. For his pains were a deed, performed once through the motion of love; but his love was without beginning and is and ever will be without any end.

# 12

And suddenly, as I looked at the same cross, he changed to an appearance of joy. The change in his appearance changed mine, and I was as glad and joyful as I could possibly be. And then cheerfully our Lord suggested to my mind: Where is there any instant of your pain or of your grief? And I was very joyful.

Then our Lord put a question to me: Are you well satisfied that I suffered for you? Yes, good Lord, I said; all my thanks to you, good Lord, blessed may you be! If you are satisfied, our Lord said, I am satisfied. It is a joy and a bliss and an endless delight to me that ever I suffered my Passion for you, for if I could suffer more, I would. In response to this, my understanding was lifted up into heaven, and there I saw three heavens; and at this sight I was greatly astonished, and I thought: I have seen three heavens, and all are of the blessed humanity of Christ. And none is greater, none is less, none is higher, none is lower, but all are equal in their joy.

For the first heaven, Christ showed me his Father, not in any corporeal likeness, but in his attributes and in his joy. For the Father's operation is this: he rewards his Son, Jesus Christ. This gift and this reward is so joyful to Jesus that his Father could have given him no reward which could have pleased him better. For the first heaven, which is the Father's bliss, appeared to me as a heaven, and it was full of bliss. For Jesus has great joy in all the deeds which he has done for our salvation, and therefore we are his, not only through our redemption but also by his Father's courteous gift. We are his bliss, we are his reward, we are his honor, we are his crown.

What I am describing now is so great a joy to Jesus that he counts as nothing his labor and his bitter sufferings and his cruel and shameful death. And in these words: If I could suffer more, I would suffer more, I saw truly that if he could die as often as once for every man who is to be saved, as he did once for all men, love would never let him rest till he had done it. And when he had done it, he would count it all as nothing for love, for everything seems only little to him in comparison with his love. And that he plainly said to me, gravely saying this: If I could suffer more. He did not say: If it were necessary to suffer more, but: If I could suffer more; for although it might not be necessary, if he could suffer more he would suffer more. This deed and this work for our salvation were as well done as he could devise it. It was done as honorably as Christ could do it, and in this I saw complete joy in Christ; but his joy would not have been complete if the deed could have been done any better than it was. And in these three sayings: It is a joy, a bliss, and an endless delight to me, there were shown to me three heavens, and in this way. By "joy" I understood that the Father was pleased, by "bliss" that the Son was honored, and by "endless delight" the Holy Spirit. The Father is pleased, the Son is honored, the Holy Spirit takes delight. Jesus wants us to pay heed to this bliss for our salvation which is in the blessed Trinity, and to take equal delight, through his grace, while we are here. And this was shown to me when he said: Are you well satisfied? And by what Christ next said: If you are satisfied, I am satisfied, he made me understand that it was as if he had said: This is joy and delight enough for me, and I ask nothing else for my labor but that I may satisfy you. Generously and completely was this revealed to me.

So think wisely, how great this saying is: That ever I suffered my Passion for you; for in that saying was given exalted understanding of the love and the delight that he had in our salvation.

# 13

Very merrily and gladly our Lord looked into his side, and he gazed and said this: See how I loved you; as if he had said: My child, if you cannot look on my divinity, see here how I suffered my side to be opened and my heart to be split in two and to send our blood and water, all that was in it; and this is a delight to me, and I wish it to be so for you.

Our Lord showed this to me to make us glad and merry. And with the same joyful appearance he looked down on his right, and brought to my mind where our Lady stood at the time of his Passion, and he said: Do you wish to see her? And I answered and said: Yes, good Lord, great thanks, if it be your will. Often times I had prayed for this, and I expected to see her in a bodily likeness; but I did not see her so. And Jesus, saying this, showed me a spiritual vision of her. Just as before I had seen her small and simple, now he showed her high and noble and glorious and more pleasing to him than all creatures. And so he wishes it to be known that all who take delight in him should take delight in her, and in the delight that he has in her and she in him. And when Jesus said: Do you wish to see her? it seemed to me that I had the greatest delight that he could have given me in this spiritual vision of her which he gave me. For our Lord showed me no particular person except our Lady, Saint Mary, and he showed her to me on three occasions. The first was as she conceived, the second was as she had been in her sorrow under the cross, and the third as she is now, in delight, honor, and joy.

And after this our Lord showed himself to me, and he appeared to me more glorified than I had seen him before, and in this I was taught that every contemplative soul to whom it is given to look and to seek will see Mary and pass on to God through contemplation. And after this teaching, simple, courteous, joyful, again and again our Lord said to me: I am he who is highest. I am he whom you love. I am he in whom you delight. I am he whom you serve. I am he for whom you long. I am he whom you desire. I am he whom you intend. I am he who is all. I am he whom Holy Church preaches and teaches to you. I am he who showed himself before to you. I repeat these words only as that every man may accept them as our Lord intended them, according to the grace God gives him in understanding and love.

And after this our Lord brought to my mind the longing that I had for him before; and I saw that nothing hindered me but sin, and I saw that this is true of us all in general, and it seemed to me that if there had been no sin, we should all have been pure and as like our Lord as he created us. And so in my folly before this time I often wondered why, through the great and prescient wisdom of God, sin was not prevented; for it seemed to me that then all would have been well.

The impulse to think this was greatly to be shunned; and I mourned and sorrowed on this account, unreasonably, lacking discretion, filled with pride. Nonetheless in this vision Jesus informed me about everything needful to me. I do not say that I need no more instruction, for after he revealed this our Lord entrusted me to Holy Church, and I am hungry and thirsty and needy and sinful and frail, and willingly submit myself among all my fellow Christians to the teaching of Holy Church to the end of my life.

He answered with these words, and said: Sin is necessary. In the word "sin," our Lord brought generally to my mind all which is not good: the shameful contempt and the complete denial of himself which he endured for us in this life and in his death, and all the pains and passions, spiritual and bodily, of all his creatures. For we are all in part denied, and we ought to be denied, following our master Jesus until we are fully purged, that is to say until we have completely denied our own mortal flesh and all our inward affections which are not good.

And the beholding of this, with all the pains that ever were or ever will be—and of all this I understood Christ's Passion for the greatest and surpassing pain—was shown to me in an instant, and quickly turned into consolation. For our good Lord God would not have the soul frightened by this ugly sight. But I did not see sin, for I believe that it has no kind of substance, no share in being, nor can it be recognized except by the pains which it causes. And it seems to me that this pain is something for a time, for it purges us and makes us know ourselves and ask for mercy; for the Passion of our Lord is comfort to us against all this, and that is his blessed will for all who will be saved. He comforts readily and sweetly with his words, and says: But all will be well, and every kind of thing will be well.

These words were revealed very tenderly, showing no kind of blame to me or to anyone who will be saved. So it would be most unkind of me to blame God or marvel at him on account of my sins, since he does not blame me for sin. So I saw how Christ has compassion on us because of sin; and just as I was before filled full of pain and compassion on account of Christ's Passion, so I was now in a measure filled with compassion for all my fellow Christians, and then I saw that every kind of compassion which one has for one's fellow Christians in love is Christ in us.

# 14

But I shall study upon this, contemplating it generally, heavily and mournfully, saying in intention to our Lord with very great fear: Ah, good Lord, how could all things be well, because of the great harm which has come through sin to your creatures? And I wished, so far as I dared, for some plainer explanation through which my mind might be at ease about this matter. And to this our blessed Lord answered, very meekly and with a most loving manner, and he showed me that Adam's sin was the greatest harm ever done or ever to be done until the end of the world. And he also showed me that this is plainly known to all Holy Church upon earth.

Furthermore, he taught me that I should contemplate his glorious atonement, for this atoning is more pleasing to the blessed divinity and more honorable for man's salvation, without comparison, than ever Adam's sin was harmful. So then it is our blessed Lord's intention in this teaching that we should pay heed to this: For since I have set right the greatest of harms, it is my will that you should know through this that I shall set right everything which is less.

He gave me understanding of two portions. One portion is our savior and our salvation. This blessed portion is open and clear and fair and bright and plentiful, for all men who are or will be of good will are comprehended in this portion. We are bidden to this by God, and drawn and counseled and taught, inwardly by the Holy Spirit and outwardly, through the grace of the same Spirit, by Holy Church. Our Lord wants us to be occupied in this, rejoicing in him, for he rejoices in us. And the more plentifully we accept this with reverence and humility, the more do we deserve thanks from him, and the more profit do we win for ourselves; and so we may rejoice and say: Our portion is our Lord.

The other portion is closed to us and hidden, that is to say all which is additional to our salvation. For this is our Lord's privy counsel, and it is fitting to God's royal dominion to keep his privy counsel in peace, and it is fitting to his subjects out of obedience and respect not to wish to know his counsel.

Our Lord has pity and compassion on us because some creatures occupy themselves so much in this; and I am certain that if we knew how much we should please him and solace ourselves by leaving it alone, we should do so. The saints in heaven wish to know nothing but what our Lord wishes to show them, and furthermore their love and their desire is governed according to our Lord's will; and so we ought to wish to be like him. And then we shall not wish or desire anything but the will of our Lord, for we are all one in God's intention.

And in this I was taught that we shall rejoice only in our blessed savior Jesus, and trust in him for everything.

## 15

As so our good Lord answered to all the questions and doubts which I could raise, saying most comfortingly in this fashion: I will make all things well, I shall make all things well, I may make all things well, and I can make all things well; and you will see that yourself, that all things will be well. When he says that he "may," I understand this to apply to the Father; and when he says that he "can," I understand this for the Son; and when he says "I will," I understand this for the Holy Spirit; and when he says "I shall," I understand this for the unity of the blessed Trinity, three persons in one truth; and when he says "You will see yourself," I understand this for the union of all men who will be saved in the blessed Trinity.

And in these five words God wishes to be enclosed in rest and in peace. And so Christ's spiritual thirst has an end. For his spiritual thirst is his longing in love, and that persists and always will until we see him on the day of judgment; for we who shall be saved and shall be Christ's joy and bliss are still here, and shall be until that day. Therefore his thirst is this incompleteness of his joy, that he does not now possess us in himself as wholly as he then will.

All this was shown to me as a revelation of his compassion, for on the day of judgment it will cease. So he has pity and compassion on us and he longs to possess us, but his wisdom and his love do not permit the end to come until the best time. And in these same five words said before: "I may make all things well," I understand powerful consolation from all the deeds of our Lord which are still to be performed; for just as the blessed Trinity created everything from nothing, just so the same blessed Trinity will make well all things which are not well. It is God's will that we pay great heed to all the deeds which he has performed, for he wishes us to know from them all which he will do; and he revealed that to me by those words which he said: And you will see yourself that every kind of thing will be well. I understand this in two ways: one is that I am well content that I do not know it; and the other is that I am glad and joyful because I shall know it. It is God's will that we should know in general that all will be well, but it is not God's will that we should know it now except as it applies to us for the present, and that is the teaching of Holy Church.

# 16

God showed me the very great delight that he has in all men and women who accept, firmly and humbly and reverently, the preaching and teaching of Holy Church, for he is Holy Church. For he is the foundation, he is the substance, he is the teaching, he is the teacher, he is the end, he is the reward for which every faithful soul labors; and he is known and will be known to every soul to whom the Holy Spirit declares this. And I am certain that all who seek in this way will prosper, for they are seeking God.

All this which I have now said and more which I shall presently say is solace against sin; for when I first saw that God does everything which is done, I did not see sin, and then I saw that all is well. But when God did show me sin, it was then that he said: All will be well.

And when almighty God had shown me his goodness

so plenteously and fully, I wished to know, concerning a certain person whom I loved, what her future would be; and by wishing this I impeded myself, for I was not then told this. And then I was answered in my reason, as it were by a friendly man: Accept it generally, and contemplate the courtesy of your Lord God as he reveals it to you, for it is more honor to God to contemplate him in all things than in any one special thing. I agreed, and with that I learned that it is more honor to God to know everything in general than it is to take delight in any special thing. And if I were to act wisely, in accordance with this teaching, I should not be glad because of any special thing or be distressed by anything at all, for all will be well.

God brought to my mind that I should sin; and because of the delight that I had in contemplating him, I did not at once pay attention to this revelation. And our Lord very courteously waited until I was ready to attend, and then our Lord brought to my mind, along with my sins, the sins of all my fellow Christians, all in general and none in particular.

# 17

Although our Lord revealed to me that I should sin, I understood everything to apply only to me. In this I conceived a gentle fear, and in answer to this our Lord said: I protect you very safely. This was said to me with more love and assurance of protection for my soul than I can or may tell. For just as it was first revealed to me that I should sin, so was consolation revealed to me—assurance of protection for all my fellow Christians. What can make me love my fellow Christians more than to see in God that he loves all who will be saved, all of them as it were one soul? And in each soul which will be saved there is a good will which never assented to sin and never will. For as there is an animal will in the lower part which cannot will any good, so there is a good will in the higher part which cannot will any evil, but always good, just as the persons of the blessed Trinity. And our Lord revealed this to me in the completeness of his love, that we are standing in his sight, yes, that he loves us now while we are here as well as he will when we are there, before his blessed face.

God also showed me that sin is no shame, but honor to man, for in this vision my understanding was lifted up into heaven; and then there came truly to my mind David, Peter and Paul, Thomas of India and Mary Magdalen, how they are known, with their sins, to their honor in the Church on earth. And it is to them no shame that they have sinned—shame is no more in the bliss of heaven—for there the tokens of sin are turned into honors. Just so our Lord showed them to me as examples of all who will come there. Sin is the sharpest scourge with which any chosen soul can be beaten, and this scourge belabors and breaks men and women, and they become so despicable in their own sight that it seems to them that they are fit for nothing but as it were to sink into hell; but when by the inspiration of the Holy Spirit contrition seizes them, then the Spirit turns bitterness into hope of God's mercy. And then the wounds begin to heal and the soul to revive, restored to the life of Holy Church. The Holy Spirit leads him to confession, willing to reveal his sins, nakedly and truthfully, with great sorrow and great shame that he has so befouled God's fair image. Then he accepts the penance for every

sin imposed by his confessor, for this is established in Holy
Church by the teaching of the Holy Spirit. Every sinful
soul must be healed by this medicine, especially of the sins
which are mortal to him. Though he be healed, his wounds
are not seen by God as wounds but as honors. And as sin
is punished here with sorrow and penance, in contrary
fashion it will be rewarded in heaven by the courteous love
of our Lord God almighty, who does not wish anyone who
comes there to lose his labors.

That reward, which we shall receive there, will not be
small, but it will be high, glorious, and honorable. And so
all shame will be turned into honor and into greater joy.
And I am sure by what I feel myself that the more that
every loving soul perceives this in the gentle and courteous
love of God, the more he will hate to sin.

# 18

But if you be moved to say or think: Since this is true, it
would be good to sin so as to have more reward, beware
of this prompting and despise it, because it comes from the
devil. For any soul who deliberately assents to this
prompting cannot be saved until he be absolved as though
from mortal sin. For if all the pain there is, in hell, in purgatory, on earth, death and other sufferings, were laid before me, together with sin, I should rather choose all that
pain than sin. For sin is so vile and so much to be hated
that it cannot be compared with any pain which is not sin.
For everything is good, except sin, and nothing is wicked,
except sin. Sin is neither death nor delight, but when a soul
deliberately chooses sin, which is pain, to be his god, in

the end he has nothing at all. That pain seems to me the cruelest hell, because the soul has not his God. A soul may have God in every pain, but not in sin.

And God's will to save man is as great as his power and his wisdom to save him. For Christ himself is the foundation of all the laws of Christian men, and he has taught us to do good against evil. Here we may see that he himself is this love, and does to us as he teaches us to do; for he wishes us to be like him, in a unity of undying love for ourselves and for our fellow Christians. No more than is his love for us withheld because of our sin does he want us to withhold our love for ourselves and our fellow Christians; we must hate sin utterly, and love souls endlessly as God loves them. For what God said is an endless strengthening, which protects us very safely.

## 19

After this our Lord revealed to me about prayers. I saw two conditions in those who pray, according to what I have felt myself. One is that they will not pray for anything at all but for the thing which is God's will and to his glory; another is that they apply themselves always and with all their might to entreat the thing which is his will and to his glory. And that is what I have understood from the teaching of Holy Church; for this is what our Lord too taught me now, to accept faith, hope, and love as gifts from God, and for us to preserve ourselves in them to the end of life. For this we say the Our Father, Hail Mary, I Believe, with such devotion as God will give us. And so we pray for all our fellow Christians, and for every kind of person as God wishes, for it is our wish that every kind of man and woman might be in the same state of virtue and grace as we ought to wish for ourselves. But still in all this, often our trust is not complete, for we are not certain that almighty God hears us, because of our unworthiness, it seems to us, and because we are feeling nothing at all; for often we are as barren and dry after our prayers as we were before. And thus when we feel so, it is our folly which is the cause of our weakness, for I have experienced this in myself. And our Lord brought all this suddenly to my mind, and gave me great strength and vitality to combat this kind of weakness in praying, and said: I am the foundation of your beseeching. First, it is my will that you should have it, and then I make you to wish it, and then I make you beseech it. And if you beseech, how could it be that you would not have what you beseech? And so in the first reason and in the three that follow it our Lord revealed a great strengthening.

Firstly, where he says: If you beseech, he shows his great delight and the everlasting reward that he will give us for our beseeching. And in the fourth reason, where he says: How could it be that you would not have what you beseech? he conveys a serious rebuke, because we have not the firm trust which we need. So our Lord wants us both to pray and to trust, for the reasons I have repeated were given to strengthen us against weakness in our prayers. For it is God's will that we pray, and he moves us to do so in these words I have told, for he wants us to be certain that our prayers are answered, because prayer pleases God. Prayers make a praying man pleased with himself, and make the man serious and humble who before this was contending and striving against himself. Prayer unites the soul to God, for although the soul may always be like God in nature and substance, it is often unlike him in condition, through human sin. Prayer makes the soul like God when the soul wills as God wills; then it is like God in condition, as it is in nature. And so he teaches us to pray and to have firm trust that we shall have what we pray for, because everything which is done would be done, even though we had never prayed for it. But God's love is so great that he regards us as partners in his good work; and so he moves us to pray for what it pleases him to do, for whatever prayer or good desire comes to us by his gift he will repay us for, and give us eternal reward. And this was revealed to me when he said: If you beseech it.

In this saying God showed me his great pleasure and great delight, as though he were much beholden to us for each good deed that we do, even though it is he who does it. Therefore we pray much that he may do what is pleasing to him, as if he were to say: How could you please me more than by entreating me, earnestly, wisely, sincerely, to do the thing that is my will? And so prayer makes harmony between God and man's soul, because when man is at ease with God he does not need to pray, but to contemplate reverently what God says. For in all the time when this was revealed to me, I was not moved to pray, but always to keep this good in my mind for my strength, that when we see God we have what we desire, and then we do not need to pray. But when we do not see God, then we need to pray, because we are failing, and for the strengthening of ourselves, to Jesus. For when a soul is tempted, troubled, and left to itself in its unrest, that is the time for it to pray and to make itself simple and obedient to God. Unless the soul be obedient, no kind of prayer makes God supple to it; for God's love does not change, but during the time that a man is in sin he is so weak, so foolish, so unloving that he can love neither God nor himself.

His greatest harm is his blindness, because he cannot see all this. Then almighty God's perfect love, which never changes, gives him sight of himself; and then he believes that God may be angry with him because of his sin. And then he is moved to contrition and, through confession and other good deeds, to appease God's anger, till he finds rest of soul and ease of conscience; and then it seems to him that God has forgiven his sins, and this is true. And then it seems to the soul that God has been moved to look upon it, as though it had been in pain or in prison, saying: I am glad that you have found rest, for I have always loved you and I love you now, and you love me. And so with prayers, as I have said, and with other good works that Holy Church teaches us to practice, the soul is united to God.

# 20

Before this time I had often great longing, and desired of God's gift to be delivered from this world and this life, for I wanted to be with my God in the bliss in which I surely hope to be without end. For often I beheld the woe that there is here, and the good and the blessed life that is there; and if there had been no other pain on earth except the absence of our Lord God, it seemed to me sometimes that that would be more than I could bear. And this made me mourn and diligently long.

Then God said to me, for my patience and endurance:

Suddenly you will be taken out of all your pain, all your unrest, and all your woe. And you will come up above, and you will have me for your reward, and you will be filled full of joy and bliss, and you will never have any kind of pain, any kind of sickness, any kind of displeasure, any kind of disappointment, but always endless joy and bliss. Why then should it grieve you to endure for a while, since it is my will and to my glory?

As God reasoned with me—"Suddenly you will be taken"—I saw how he rewards men for their patience in awaiting the time of his will, and how men have patience to endure throughout the span of their lives, because they do not know when the time for them to die will come. This is very profitable, because if they knew when that would be, they would set a limit to their patience. Then, too, it is God's will that so long as the soul is in the body, it should seem to a man that he is always on the point of being taken. For all this life and all the longing we have here is only an instant of time, and when we are suddenly taken into bliss out of pain, it will be nothing.

Therefore our Lord said: Why then should it grieve you to endure for a while, since that is my will and to my glory? It is God's will that we accept his commands and his consolations as generously and as fully as we are able; and he also wants us to accept our tarrying and our suffering as lightly as we are able, and to count them as nothing. For the more lightly we accept them, the less importance we ascribe to them because of our love, the less pain shall we experience from them and the more thanks shall we have for them.

In this blessed revelation I was truly taught that any man or woman who voluntarily chooses God in his lifetime may be sure that he too is chosen. Pay true heed to this, for it is indeed God's will for us to be as certain in our trust to have the bliss of heaven whilst we are here as we shall be certain of it when we are there.

And always, the more delight and joy that we accept from this certainty, with reverence and humility, the more pleasing is it to God. For I am certain that if there had been no one but I to be saved, God would have done everything which he has done for me. And so ought every soul to think, acknowledging who it is who loves him, forgetting if he can the rest of creation, and thinking that God has done everything he has done for him. And it seems to me that this ought to move a soul to love him and delight in him, and to fear nothing but him; for it is his will that we know that all the power of our enemy is shut in the hand of our friend. And therefore a soul that knows this to be sure will fear nothing but him whom he loves, and count all other fears among the sufferings and bodily sicknesses and illusions which he must endure.

And therefore if a man be in so much pain, so much woe, and so much unrest that it seems to him that he can think of nothing at all but the state he is in or what he is feeling, let him, as soon as he may, pass it over lightly and count it as nothing. Why? Because God wants to be known; and because if we knew him and loved him we should have patience and be in great rest, and all that he does would be a delight to us. And our Lord revealed this to me by his words, when he said: Why then should it grieve you to endure for a while, since that is my will and to my glory? And here came the end of all that our Lord revealed to me on that day.

# 21

And after this I soon fell back to myself and to my bodily sickness, understanding that I should live, and as the wretched creature that I am, I grieved and mourned for the bodily pains which I felt, and thought how irksome it was that I must go on living. And I was as barren and dry as if the consolation which I had received before were trifling, because my pains had returned and my spiritual perceptions failed.

Then a man of religion came to me and asked me how I did, and I said that during the day I had been raving. And he laughed aloud and heartily. And I said: The cross that stood at the foot of my bed bled profusely; and when I said this, the religious I was speaking to became very serious and surprised. And at once I was very ashamed of my imprudence, and I thought: This man takes seriously every word I could say, and he says nothing in reply. And when I saw that he treated it so seriously and so respectfully, I was greatly ashamed, and wanted to make my confession. But I could not tell it to any priest, for I thought: How could a priest believe me? I did not believe our Lord God. I believed this truly at the time when I saw him, and it was then my will and my intention to do so forever. But like a fool I let it pass from my mind.

See what a wretched creature I am! This was a great sin and a great ingratitude, that I was so foolish, because of a little bodily pain that I felt, as to abandon so imprudently the strength of all this blessed revelation from our Lord God. Here you can see what I am in myself; but our courteous Lord would not leave me so. And I lay still until night, trusting in his mercy, and then I began to sleep.

And as soon as I fell asleep, it seemed to me that the devil set himself at my throat and wanted to strangle me, but he could not. And I awoke, more dead than alive. The people who were with me watched me, and wet my temples, and my heart began to gain strength. And then a little smoke came in at the door, with great heat and a foul stench. I said: Blessed be the Lord! Is everything on fire here? And I thought that it must be actual fire, which would have burned us to death. I asked those who were with me if they were conscious of any stench. They said no, they were not. I said: Blessed be God! for then I knew well that it was the devil who had come to assail me. And at once I assented to all that our Lord had revealed to me on that same day, and to all the faith of Holy Church, for I consider them both to be one, and I fled to them as to my source of strength. And immediately everything vanished, and I was enabled to have rest and peace, without bodily sickness or fear of conscience.

# 22

But I lay still awake, and then our Lord opened my spiritual eyes, and showed me my soul in the midst of my heart. I saw my soul as wide as if it were a kingdom, and from the state which I saw in it, it seemed to me as if it were a fine city. In the midst of this city sits our Lord Jesus, true God and true man, a handsome person and tall, honorable, the greatest lord. And I saw him splendidly clad in honors. He sits erect there in the soul, in peace and rest, and he rules and he guards heaven and earth and everything that is. The humanity and the divinity sit at rest, and the divinity rules and guards, without instrument or effort. And my soul is blessedly occupied by the divinity, sovereign power, sovereign wisdom, sovereign goodness.

The place which Jesus takes in our soul he will nevermore vacate, for in us is his home of homes, and it is the greatest delight for him to dwell there. This was a delectable and a restful sight, for it is so in truth forevermore; and to contemplate this while we are here is most pleasing to God, and very great profit to us. And the soul who thus contemplates is made like to him who is contemplated, and united to him in rest and peace. And it was a singular joy and bliss to me that I saw him sit, for the contemplation of this sitting revealed to me the certainty that he will dwell in us forever; and I knew truly that it was he who had revealed everything to me before. And when I had contemplated this with great attention, our Lord very humbly revealed words to me, without voice and without opening of lips, as he had done before, and said very seriously: Know it well, it was no raving, which you saw today, but accept and believe it and hold firmly to it, and you will not be overcome.

These last words were said to me to teach me perfect certainty that it is our Lord Jesus who revealed everything to me; for just as in the first words which our Lord revealed to me, alluding to his blessed Passion, "With this the fiend is overcome," just so he said with perfect certainty in these last words, "You will not be overcome." And this teaching and this true strengthening apply generally to all my fellow Christians, as I have said before, and so is the will of God.

And these words, "You will not be overcome," were said very insistently and strongly, for certainty and strength against every tribulation which may come. He did not say: You will not be assailed, you will not be belabored, you will not be disquieted, but he said: You will not be overcome. God wants us to pay attention to his words, and always to be strong in our certainty, in well-being and in woe, for he loves us and delights in us, and so he wishes us to love him and delight in him and trust greatly in him, and all will be well.

And soon afterward all was hidden, and I saw no more.

# 23

After this the devil returned with his heat and his stench, and kept me very busy. The stench was vile and painful, and the physical heat was fearful and oppressive; and I could also hear in my ears chattering and talking, as if between two speakers, and they seemed to be both chattering at once, as if they were conducting a confused debate, and it was all low muttering. And I did not understand what they said, but all this, it seemed, was to move me to despair; and I kept on trusting in God, and spoke words aloud to comfort my soul, as I should have done to another person who was so belabored. It seemed to me that this commotion could not be compared with anything on earth. I fixed my eyes on the same cross in which I had seen comfort before, and I occupied my tongue in speaking of Christ's Passion and in repeating the faith of Holy Church, and I fixed my heart on God with all the trust and the strength that was in me. And I thought privately to myself: Now you have plenty to do; if from now on you would be so busy in keeping yourself free of sin, that would be a most excellent occupation. For I truly believe that if I were safe from sin I should be very safe from all the devils of hell and the enemies of my soul.

And so they occupied me all that night and into the morning, until it was a little after sunrise; and then all at once they had all gone and disappeared, leaving nothing but their stench, and that persisted for a little while. And I despised them, and so I was delivered from them by the strength of Christ's Passion. For it is so that the fiend is overcome, as Christ said before to me.

O, wretched sin, what are you? You are nothing. For I saw that God is in everything; I did not see you. And when I saw that God had made everything, I did not see you. And when I saw that God is in everything, I did not see you. And when I saw that God does everything that is done, the less and the greater, I did not see you. And when I saw our Lord Jesus Christ seated in our soul so honorably, and love and delight and rule and guard all that he has made, I did not see you. And so I am certain that you are nothing, and all those who love you and delight you and follow you and deliberately end in you, I am sure that they will be brought to nothing with you and eternally confounded. Amen, for love of him.

And I wish to say what wretchedness is, as I am taught by God's revelation. Wretchedness is everything which is not good, the spiritual blindness that we fall into by our first sin, and all that follows from that wretchedness, sufferings and pains, spiritual or physical, and everything on earth or elsewhere which is not good. And then concerning this it may be asked: What are we? and to this I answer: If everything were separated from us which is not good, we should be good. When wretchedness is separated from us, God and the soul are wholly at unity and God and man are wholly one. What is everything on earth which divides us? I answer and say that in the respect in which it serves us it is good, and in the respect in which it will perish it is wretchedness, and in the respect that a man sets his heart upon it otherwise than thus it is sin. And so long as man or woman loves sin, if there be such, he is in pain beyond all pains; and when he does not love sin, but hates it and loves God, all is well. And he who truly does so, though sometimes he sin through weakness or ignorance in his will, he does not fall, because he wishes to exert himself to rise again and look upon God, whom he loves in all his will. God has made things to be loved by men or women who have been sinners; but always he loves and longs to have our love, and when we have a strong and wise love for Jesus, we are at peace.

All the blessed teaching of our Lord God was shown to me in three parts, as I have said before, that is to say by bodily vision, and by words formed in my understanding, and by spiritual vision. About the bodily vision I have said as I saw, as truly as I am able. And about the words formed, I have repeated them just as our Lord revealed them to me. And about the spiritual vision, I have told a part, but I can never tell it in full; and therefore I am moved to say more about this spiritual vision, as God will give me grace.

# 24

God showed me two kinds of sickness that we have, of which he wants us to be cured. One is impatience, because we bear our labor and our pain heavily. The other is despair, coming from doubtful fear, as I shall say afterward. And it is these two which most belabor and assail us, by what our Lord showed me, and it is most pleasing to him that they should be amended. I am speaking of such men and women as for the love of God hate sin and dispose themselves to do God's will. So these are two secret sins, extremely busy in tempting us. Therefore it is God's will that they should be known, and then we shall reject them as we do other sins.

And so very meekly our Lord showed me what patience he had in his cruel Passion, and also the joy and delight that he has in that Passion, because of love. And he showed me this as an example of how we ought gladly and easily to bear our pains, for that is very pleasing to him and an endless profit to us. And the reason why we are oppressed by them is because of our ignorance of love. Though the persons of the blessed Trinity be all alike in their attributes, it was their love which was most shown to me, and that it is closest to us all. And it is about this knowledge that we are most blind, for many men and women believe that God is almighty and may do everything, and that he is all wisdom and can do everything, but that he is all love and wishes to do everything, that is where they fail. And it is this ignorance which most hinders God's lovers, for when they begin to hate sin and to amend themselves according to the laws of Holy Church, still there persists a fear which moves them to look at themselves and their sins committed in the past. And they take this fear for humility, but it is a reprehensible blindness and weakness; and we do not know how to despise it, as we should at once despise it, like any other sin which we recognize, if we knew it for what it is, because it comes from the enemy, and it is contrary to truth. For of all the attributes of the blessed Trinity, it is God's will that we have most confidence in his delight and his love.

For love makes power and wisdom very humble to us; for just as by God's courtesy he forgets our sin from the time that we repent, just so does he wish us to forget our sins and all our depression and all our doubtful fears.

# 25

For I saw four kinds of fear. One is fear of assault, which comes to a man suddenly through timidity. This fear is good, for it helps to purge a man, as does bodily sickness or such other pains which are not sinful; for all such pains help one if they are patiently accepted. The second is fear of pain, through which a man is stirred and wakened from the sleep of sin; for anyone fast asleep in sin is not for that time able to receive the gentle strength of the Holy Spirit, until he has obtained this fear of pain and of the fire of purgatory. And this fear moves him to seek comfort and mercy of God; and so this fear helps him as though by chance, and enables him to have contrition by the blessed teaching of the Holy Spirit. The third is a doubtful fear; if it be recognized for what it is, however little it may be, it is a kind of despair. For I am certain that God hates all doubtful fear, and he wishes us to drive it out, knowing truly how we may live. The fourth is reverent fear, for there is no fear in us which pleases him but reverent fear, and that is very sweet and gentle, because our love is great. And yet this reverent fear is not the same as love; they are different in kind and in effect, and neither of them may be obtained without the other.

Therefore I am sure that he who loves, he fears, though he may feel little of this. Whatever kinds of fear be suggested to us other than reverent fear, though they appear disguised as holiness, they are not so true; and this is how they can be recognized and distinguished, one from the other. The more that one has of this reverent fear, the more it softens and strengthens and pleases and gives rest; and false fear belabors and assails and perturbs. So that the remedy is to recognize them both and to reject false fear, just as we should an evil spirit who presented himself in the likeness of a good angel. For it is so with an evil spirit; though he may come under the disguise and likeness of a good angel, with his dalliance and his operations, however fair he may appear, he first belabors and tempts and perturbs the person he speaks to, and hinders him and leaves him in great unrest; and the more he communicates with him, the more he oppresses him and the further the man is from peace. Therefore it is God's will and to our profit that we recognize them apart; for God wants us always to be strong in our love, and peaceful and restful as he is toward us, and he wants us to be, for ourselves and for our fellow Christians, what he is for us. Amen.

The end of the book of Julian of Norwich.

# THE SHOWINGS
## (LONG TEXT)

*In the long years as an anchoress that succeeded the experience described in the Short Text, Julian continued to reflect and meditate on "the Showings"—they became the core of her theology and her spirituality. Twenty years later she wrote a much longer version, which repeats most of the original text but adds some significant material. I find the longer version less immediately appealing than the short version, but it is important to note some developments in her thought—above all in her much stronger sense of the Trinity, in her deeper sense of God and of God's love (she makes the comment, original for her time, that in her view there is "no anger in God"). She continues to brood on what perhaps felt most puzzling to her, as one who had experienced the love of God—the mystery of suffering and of evil. She is very near the heretical position that hell does not exist, at least as a place where some souls will suffer to all eternity. She is obedient to the Church but she believes that "all shall be well," a conviction impossible to reconcile with eternal damnation.*

As truly as God is our Father, so truly is God our Mother, and he revealed that in everything, and especially in these sweet words where he says: I am he; that is to say: I am he, the power and goodness of fatherhood; I am he, the wisdom and the lovingness of motherhood; I am he, the light and the grace which is all blessed love; I am he, the Trinity; I am he, the unity; I am he, the great supreme goodness of every kind of thing; I am he who makes you to love; I am he who makes you to long: I am he, the endless fulfilling of all true desires. For where the soul is highest, noblest, most honorable, still it is lowest, meekest, and mildest.

And from this foundation in substance we have all the powers of our sensuality by the gift of nature, and by the help and the furthering of mercy and grace, without which we cannot profit. Our great Father, almighty God, who is being, knows us and loved us before time began. Out of this knowledge, in his most wonderful deep love, by the prescient eternal counsel of all the blessed Trinity, he wanted the second person to become our Mother, our brother, and out savior. From this it follows that as truly as God is our Father, so truly is God our Mother. Our Father wills, our Mother works, our good Lord the Holy Spirit confirms. And therefore it is our part to love our God in whom we have our being, reverently thanking and praising him for our creation, mightily praying to our Mother for mercy and pity, and to our Lord the Holy Spirit for help and grace. For in these three is all our life; nature, mercy, and grace, of which we have mildness, patience, and pity, and hatred of sin and wickedness; for the virtues must of themselves hate sin and wickedness.

And so Jesus is our true Mother in nature by our first creation, and he is our true Mother in grace by his taking our created nature. All the lovely works and all the sweet loving offices of beloved motherhood are appropriated to the second person, for in him we have this godly will, whole and safe forever, both in nature and in grace, from his own goodness proper to him.

I understand three ways of contemplating motherhood in God. The first is the foundation of our nature's creation; the second is his taking of our nature, where the motherhood of grace begins; the third is the motherhood at work. And in that, by the same grace, everything is penetrated, in length and in breadth, in height and in depth without end; and it is all one love.

But now I should say a little more about this penetration, as I understood our Lord to mean: how we are brought back by the motherhood of mercy and grace into our natural place, in which we were created by the motherhood of love, a mother's love which never leaves us.

Our Mother in nature, our Mother in grace, because he wanted altogether to become our Mother in all things, made the foundation of his work most humbly and most mildly in the maiden's womb. And he revealed that in the first revelation, when he brought that meek maiden before the eye of my understanding in the simple stature which she had when she conceived; that is to say that our great God, the supreme wisdom of all things, arrayed and prepared himself in this humble place, all ready in our poor flesh, himself to do the service and the office of motherhood in everything. The mother's service is nearest, readiest, and surest: nearest because it is most natural, readiest because it is most loving, and surest because it is truest. No one ever might or could perform this office fully, except only him. We know that all our mothers bear us for pain and for death. Oh, what is that? But our true Mother Jesus, he alone bears us for joy and for endless life, blessed may he be. So he carries us within him in love and travail, until the full time when he wanted to suffer the sharpest thorns and cruel pains that ever were or will be, and at the last he died. And when he had finished and had borne us so for bliss, still all this could not satisfy his wonderful love. And he revealed this in these great surpassing words of love: If I could suffer more, I would suffer more. He could not die any more, but he did not want to cease working; therefore he must needs nourish us, for the precious love of motherhood has made him our debtor.

The mother can give her child to suck of her milk, but

our precious Mother Jesus can feed us with himself, and does, most courteously and most tenderly, with the blessed sacrament, which is the precious food of true life; and with all the sweet sacraments he sustains us most mercifully and graciously, and so he meant in these blessed words, where he said: I am he whom Holy Church preaches and teaches to you. That is to say: All the health and the life of the sacraments, all the power and the grace of my word, all the goodness which is ordained in Holy Church for you, I am he.

The mother can lay her child tenderly to her breast, but our tender Mother Jesus can lead us easily into his blessed breast through his sweet open side, and show us there a part of the godhead and of the joys of heaven, with inner certainty of endless bliss. And that he revealed in the tenth revelation, giving us the same understanding in these sweet words which he says: See, how I love you, looking into his blessed side, rejoicing.

This fair lovely word "mother" is so sweet and so kind in itself that it cannot truly be said of anyone or to anyone except of him and to him who is the true Mother of life and of all things. To the property of motherhood belong nature, love, wisdom, and knowledge, and this is God. For though it may be so that our bodily bringing to birth is only little, humble, and simple in comparison with our spiritual bringing to birth, still it is he who does it in the creatures by whom it is done. The kind, loving mother who knows and sees the need of her child guards it very tenderly, as the nature and condition of motherhood will have. And always as the child grows in age and stature, she acts differently, but she does not change her love. And when it is even older, she allows it to be chastised to destroy its faults, so as to make the child receive virtues and grace. This work, with everything which is lovely and good, our Lord performs in those by whom it is done. So he is our Mother in nature by the operation of grace in the lower part, for love of the higher part. And he wants us to know it, for he wants to have all our love attached to him; and in this I saw that every debt which we owe by God's command to fatherhood and motherhood is fulfilled in truly loving God, which blessed love Christ works in us. And this was revealed in everything, and especially in the great bounteous words when he says: I am he whom you love.

And in our spiritual bringing to birth he uses more tenderness, without any comparison, in protecting us. By so much as our soul is more precious in his sight, he kindles our understanding, he prepares our ways, he eases our conscience, he comforts our soul, he illumines our heart and gives us partial knowledge and love of his blessed divinity, with gracious memory of his sweet humanity and his blessed Passion, with courteous wonder over his great surpassing goodness, and makes us to love everything which he loves for love of him, and to be well satisfied with him and with all his works. And when we fall, quickly he raises us up with his loving embrace and his gracious touch. And when we are strengthened by his sweet working, then we willingly choose him by his grace, that we shall be his servants and his lovers, constantly and forever.

And yet after this he allows some of us to fall more heavily and more grievously than ever we did before, as it seems to us. And then we who are not all wise think that everything which we have undertaken was all nothing. But it is not so, for we need to fall, and we need to see it; for if we did not fall, we should not know how feeble and how wretched we are in ourselves, nor, too, should we know so completely the wonderful love of our Creator.

For we shall truly see in heaven without end that we have sinned grievously in this life; and notwithstanding this, we shall truly see that we were never hurt in his love, nor were we ever of less value in his sight. And by the experience of this falling we shall have a great and marvelous knowledge of love in God without end; for enduring and marvelous is that love which cannot and will not be broken because of offenses.

And this was one profitable understanding; another is the humility and meekness which we shall obtain by the sight of our fall, for by that we shall be raised high in heaven, to which raising we might never have come without that meekness. And therefore we need to see it; and if we do not see it, though we fell, that would not profit us. And commonly we first fall and then see it; and both are from the mercy of God.

The mother may sometimes suffer the child to fall and to be distressed in various ways, for its own benefit, but she can never suffer any kind of peril to come to her child, because of her love. And though our earthly mother may suffer her child to perish, our heavenly Mother Jesus may never suffer us who are his children to perish, for he is almighty, all wisdom, and all love, and so is none but he, blessed may he be.

But often when our falling and our wretchedness are shown to us, we are so much afraid and so greatly ashamed of ourselves that we scarcely know where we can put ourselves. But then our courteous Mother does not wish us to flee away, for nothing would be less pleasing to him; but he then wants us to behave like a child. For when it is distressed and frightened, it runs quickly to its mother; and if it can do no more, it calls to the mother for help with all its might. So he wants us to act as a meek child, saying: My kind Mother, my gracious Mother, my beloved Mother, have mercy on me. I have made myself filthy and unlike you, and I may not and cannot make it right except with your help and grace.

And if we do not then feel ourselves eased, let us at once be sure that he is behaving as a wise Mother. For if he sees that it is profitable to us to mourn and to weep, with compassion and pity he suffers that until the right time has come, out of his love. And then he wants us to show a child's characteristics, which always naturally trusts in its mother's love in well-being and in woe. And he wants us to commit ourselves fervently to the faith of Holy Church, and find there our beloved Mother in consolation and true understanding, with all the company of the blessed. For one single person may often be broken, as it seems to him, but the entire body of Holy Church was never broken, nor ever will be without end. And therefore it is a certain thing, and good and gracious to will, meekly and fervently, to be fastened and united to our mother Holy Church, who is Christ Jesus. For the flood of mercy which is his dear blood and precious water is plentiful to make us fair and clean. The blessed wounds of our savior are open and rejoice to heal us. The sweet gracious hands of our Mother are ready and diligent about us; for he in all this work exercises the true office of a kind nurse, who has nothing else to do but attend to the safety of her child.

It is his office to save us, it is his glory to do it, and it is his will that we know it; for he wants us to love him sweetly and trust in him meekly and greatly. And he revealed this in these gracious words: I protect you very safely.

For at that time he revealed our frailty and our falling, our trespasses and our humiliations, our chagrins and our burdens and all our woe, as much as it seemed to me could happen in this life. And with that he revealed his blessed power, his blessed wisdom, his blessed love, and that he protects us at such times, as tenderly and as sweetly, to his glory, and as surely to our salvation as he does when we are in the greatest consolation and comfort, and raises us to this in spirit, on high in heaven, and turns everything to his glory and to our joy without end. For his precious love, he never allows us to lose time; and all this is of the natural goodness of God by the operation of grace.

God is essence in his very nature; that is to say, that goodness which is natural is God. He is the ground, his is the substance, he is very essence or nature, and he is the true Father and the true Mother of natures. And all natures which he had made to flow out of him to work his will, they will be restored and brought back into him by the salvation of man through the operation of grace. For all natures which he has put separately in different creatures are all in man, wholly, in fulness and power, in beauty and in goodness, in kingliness and in nobility, in every manner of stateliness, preciousness, and honor.

Here we can see that we are all bound to God by nature, and we are bound to God by grace. Here we can see that we do not need to seek far afield so as to know various natures, but to go to Holy Church, into our Mother's breast, that is to say, into our own soul, where our Lord dwells. And there we should find everything, now in faith and understanding, and afterward truly, in himself, clearly, in bliss.

But let no man or woman apply this particularly to himself, because it is not so. It is general, because it is our precious Mother Christ, and for him was this fair nature prepared for the honor and nobility of man's creation, and for the joy and the bliss of man's salvation, just as he saw, knew, and recognized from without beginning.

Here we may see that truly it belongs to our nature to hate sin, and truly it belongs to us by grace to hate sin; for nature is all good and fair in itself, and grace was sent out to save nature and destroy sin and bring fair nature back again to the blessed place from which it came, which is God, with more nobility and honor by the powerful operation of grace. For it will be seen before God by all his saints in joy without end that nature has been tried in the fire of tribulation, and that no lack or defect is found in it.

So are nature and grace of one accord; for grace is God, as uncreated nature is God. He is two in his manner of operation, and one in love, and neither of these works without the other, and they are not separated. And when we by the mercy of God and with his help reconcile ourselves to nature and to grace, we shall see truly that sin is incomparably worse, more vile and painful than hell. For it is in opposition to our fair nature; for as truly as sin is unclean, so truly is sin unnatural. All this is a horrible thing to see for the loving soul which would wish to be all fair and shining in the sight of God, as nature and grace teach. But do not let us be afraid of this, except insofar as fear may be profitable; but let us meekly lament to our beloved Mother, and he will sprinkle us all with his precious blood, and make our soul most pliable and most mild, and heal us most gently in the course of time, just as it is most glory to him and joy to us without end. And from this sweet and gentle operation he will never cease or desist, until all his beloved children are born and brought to birth; and he revealed that when he gave understanding of the spiritual thirst which is the longing in love which will last till the day of judgment.

So in our true Mother Jesus our life is founded in his own prescient wisdom from without beginning, with the great power of the Father and the supreme goodness of the Holy Spirit. And in accepting our nature he gave us life, and in his blessed dying on the cross he bore us to endless life. And since that time, now and ever until the day of judgment, he feeds us and fosters us, just as the great supreme lovingness of motherhood wishes, and as the natural need of childhood asks. Fair and sweet is our heavenly Mother in the sight of our soul; precious and lovely are the children of grace in the sight of our heavenly Mother, with gentleness and meekness and all the lovely virtues which belong to children by nature. For the child does not naturally despair of the mother's love, the child does not necessarily rely upon itself; naturally the child loves the mother and either of them the other.

These, and all others that resemble them, are such fair virtues, with which our heavenly Mother is served and pleased. And I understood no greater stature in this life than childhood, with its feebleness and lack of power and intelligence, until the time that our gracious Mother has brought us up into our Father's bliss. And there it will truly be made known to us what he means in the sweet words when he says: All will be well, and you will see it yourself, that every kind of thing will be well. And then will the bliss of our motherhood in Christ be to begin anew in the joys of our Father, God, which new beginnings will last, newly beginning without end.

Thanks be to God. Here ends the book of
revelations of Julian the anchorite of Norwich,
on whose soul may God have mercy.

# CREDITS